Angelos Michalopoulos

THE DREAM THAT DARED TO BECOME A MAN

Translation:

Angelos Michalopoulos, Andreas Machairas

ATHENS 2015

© Angelos Michalopoulos, 2015.
This publication (work, material, book) may not be reproduced, transmitted or copied in part or in whole, by any means and in any form, nor may it be translated, adapted, adjusted, converted, or otherwise circulated or communicated to the public in any way or by any means, in accordance with the provisions of L. 2121/1993 and the Berne Convention for the Protection of Literary and Artistic Works, without the prior written approval of the author.
The reproduction of the typesetting and layout, the cover and the overall aesthetic appearance of this book by photocopying, electronic or any other methods for purposes of exploitation is strictly prohibited according to article 51 of L. 2121/1993.

www.angelosm.com
email: onelilo@angelosm.com

ISBN: 978-618-81397-9-4

CHARACTERS:

Narrator

Paul

His self-confidence

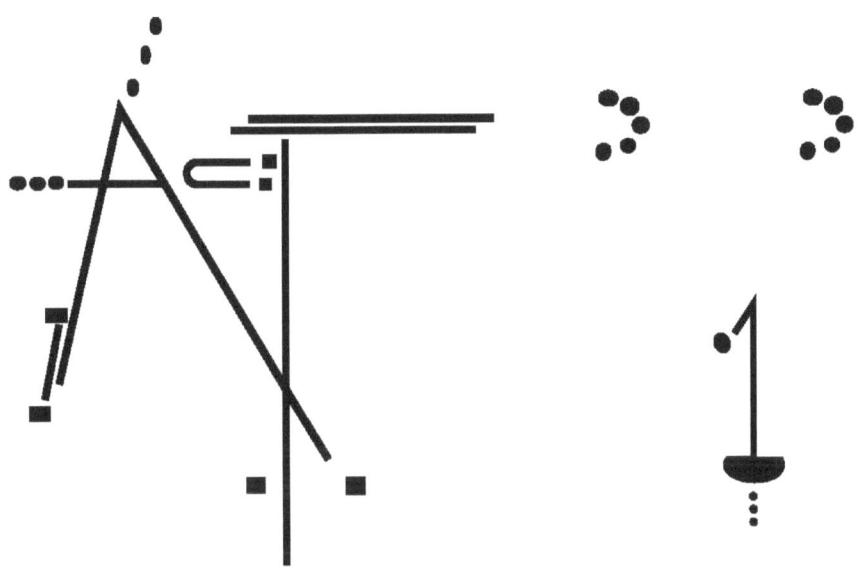

Paul and his Self-Confidence are sitting diametrically opposed on two high chairs, as far away from each other as they can.

NARRATOR: On the chess board on which man plays a game with his Self-Confidence, some of the pieces constantly find new ways to refuse to let him touch them. As they talk, the morning starts to slowly take on the aroma left behind by her as she crosses the room shredding with every step of hers a different kind of cowardice hosted in her owner's eyes. It's the time when the correct spelling of a guilt brushes past the security felt by any shortcoming of his that can still stand to look her in the eyes without fainting. The dozens of loose emotions then living in the room, some lying on the sofas, others scattered for some time now on the floor, almost forgotten, are trying to find in their reason for being a novel excuse, a different way to speak again, to say what they're not sure yet they know how to express. Is it perhaps time for him to wonder why his next word does not necessarily have to pass through his previous silence? Perhaps it is. It's a tough moment in a man's life when he figures out that all this time, without realizing it, he has been cheating on his serenity with his own shadow.

PAUL: Damn Self-Confidence of mine, too often in my life you manage to become the wall that begins every morning to rebuild itself between me and my happiness.

SELF-CONFIDENCE: No I don't. It's you, just you who creates an emotional distance between you and your happiness. Please don't blame me for something we've both known for some time now how well you can do without anyone's help, while at the same time you manage to convince yourself that you are completely uninvolved! *(Pause)* I don't know if you can see her, but an old friend, your insecurity, is standing upright at the only spot in your life that insists on permanently living across from you, smiling at you, as if trying to convey a message.

PAUL: I don't know if I'll be able to climb the uphills your next thought wants to construct in my mind.

SELF-CONFIDENCE: You will manage as long as you don't let the most faint-hearted part of your cowardice feel frightened before you do.

PAUL: I would say as long as I don't let any part of my optimism despair after I do.

SELF-CONFIDENCE: Perhaps…

PAUL: I feel as if I am sitting on the most frightened spot of my fist, trying to find the courage to introduce myself to my meaning before I am forced to introduce myself to hers. I see the leftovers of my joy that no longer want to be joyful, the ones I do my best not to toss into the trash of the day that just ended, trying to persuade me to use my hand and shove aside the storm that's coming from inside me and then pick up my favorite math notebook, the one my soul always used to prove to me how smarter than me she is, so I can figure out how much I owe you.

SELF-CONFIDENCE: If you want to measure out something, start counting how many fists you can fit in a teardrop of yours. Find the courage to unfasten any teardrop of yours you can from your soul and install it in the middle of your palm, so you can ask it the questions you should have asked your aggressiveness years ago.

PAUL: Don't go there, don't…

SELF-CONFIDENCE: Why not, why shouldn't we talk about your malice, this witch that lives inside you, the one who would like so much to convince you that she will be able to install an enormous smile in the middle of your mouth the next time you will let her spill her toxic fluid on the people around you, to make them suffer? So stop submitting to her will, or at last stop trying to find a space inside your teardrop, even a minimal space, to put the part of your intelligence that believes more in your malice than in you.

PAUL: There is no end to what doesn't know how to begin.

SELF-CONFIDENCE: No, there isn't.

PAUL: What I feel is so horrible! I feel like my tears are reversing course before they reach my eyes and unload their meaning one by one on the very emotions of mine that gave birth to them. How can a mind come up with a novel way everytime for night to fall inside it while around it's still high noon? How can it manage to fit an entire life in the day that's coming, when her owner has already presold all the week's upcoming dawns to his pessimism? I feel that the pathways of my mind are emptying of thoughts, and even more of the promises I gave them that I would start thinking them. Incensed thoughts are jumping out of every corner of my brain, heading to its center to demand their rights.

SELF-CONFIDENCE: Don't you feel that hundreds of little fires have managed to stretch a rope across the deepest crevice in your head and are struggling to balance on it, each one trying to catch up to your biggest question which has already started crossing it?

PAUL: I know, I know, you will probably quote again what has long been your favorite saying, that no one is fast enough to convince his conscience in time to go to sleep, hoping that he will manage, even for a few minutes, without her catching on, to create the thoughts he really wants to think about, the ones that she has long forbidden him to even consider thinking. He knows that if she sees him, she will immediately rush to take in hand the smartest sledgehammer at her disposal and will start bashing these very thoughts, to smash them into as many pieces as she can. She won't stop until she discovers inside them that ambitious full stop he has been trying to insert between the end of his ambiguity and the beginning of his next step, and after cornering it in her best arguments, will distort it so it won't be able to put an end to anything anymore.

SELF-CONFIDENCE: I detest those full stops whose ability to put an end has been compromised by man.

PAUL: I knew you would say that, and that's why I told you…

SELF-CONFIDENCE: Stop fooling around and listen to what the end of your courage is whispering to you when it doesn't want to cross the finish line you have set for it.

PAUL: What do you mean?

SELF-CONFIDENCE: Take a good look. Aren't you impressed by the fact that your courage has placed an old laugh of yours on its finish line and is waiting for you to step on it first and crush it?

PAUL: Please, don't force my life's joys to use asterisks when they talk to me. Not them, I wouldn't stand it. Anyway, at the end of each of my bouts with you, my shortcomings always wait for me, using the cheapest applause they have at their disposal to madly celebrate, hoping this way to make me feel better. They will wait as long as necessary, until I manage to get up from the mat, to award me a worthless plastic medal and an enormous solid gold asterisk.

SELF-CONFIDENCE: Come on, you know that every victory, after first managing to smudge the notes about herself she personally wrote down moments ago on the margins of her owners conscience, awards the winner a totally new insecurity, an insecurity which, no matter how many victories he has won in the past, he has never seen before.

PAUL: How I wish the victories in my life were emotionally pure, didn't owe anything to anyone.

SELF-CONFIDENCE: Victories are made to always be indebted.

PAUL: Is that why they never become entirely our own?

SELF-CONFIDENCE: Exactly.

PAUL: Why don't I feel the same about my defeats?

SELF-CONFIDENCE: Every man is the absolute owner of his defeats, while his victories he can only rent.

PAUL: From whom?

SELF-CONFIDENCE: From his self-confidence. *(Pause)* Don't forget that in your conscience's old notebook, the one torn by the million times you frantically turned the pages of yourself trying to find the pieces you had occasionally thrown away, deeming them the most useless, you might one day manage to fit your self-criticism, but never its questions as well. And you know what notebook I am talking about. The one you've been carrying wherever you go to be able to look up any information each time you don't know what to call your next fear, the one who's looking you in the eyes not knowing how to attack you.

PAUL: Damn me! It's true, I really panic each time I cannot quickly figure out what I am frightened of! But tell me, in which part of my world will I be able to find the key that will open the door to my soul, the one door I still haven't started constructing?

SELF-CONFIDENCE: At the spot where, while entering the first truth you'll find hiding behind your bravest lie, you will discover in you the strength to switch on the darkness before you turn on the light.

PAUL: What more can a key want to know about me before it allows me to grasp it in my hand?

SELF-CONFIDENCE: I was always amazed by the fact that the people who seem to be extremely self-confident and take huge risks in their life are the ones who, because they don't feel the need to explore their inner world, end up having at their disposal an enormous amount of energy to explore the world around them.

PAUL: Maybe because they don't feel the need to concern themselves with what's happening inside them, or even the pleasure associated with it, letting their optimism free to surge out of their bodies to go discover, to conquer. Convoluted thinking kills the optimism that decisiveness needs in order to flourish. It slows it down, it pulls it back, making it hesitate all the time. Thus people who are extremely linear inside them, people who are not willing to analyze what they are made of, people in whose minds live only thoughts that cannot bear to be complicated or, for that matter, dilemmas that aggressively demand to quickly become the next decisions, end up becoming great explorers and creative geniuses. Their own thoughts have long since tossed their doubts into the trash and most of their reservations into the sewers of their minds. You see, you can't feel confused inside you if you want to avoid being tripped by your own words, your own actions everytime you want to say or do something.

SELF-CONFIDENCE: That's right, you can't attack with all your strength, with all your heart, when you are preoccupied with questions and second thoughts. You cannot win when, besides the opponent you see before you, you see other opponents inside you who seek to start challenging you the moment the fight begins. Second thoughts create first-class defeats, defeats that always demand to be bigger, more devastating than any others. A simple thought knows how to attack, how to quickly choose an operating mode and then proceed, kicking backwards at all the "what ifs" that chase after her trying to take her aside so that each one can start explaining its point of view. A complex thought cannot decide where it will attack first and gets tangled in its own feet, and so ends up attacking using a small part of its strength, since it has already used up so much of it trying to defeat the opponents that live within you. You cannot defeat the opponents in front of you if you don't first defeat the ones that live inside you.

PAUL: Once again you have managed to dethrone my smile from my day's highest peak.

SELF-CONFIDENCE: It's not my fault. On the way to your success don't expect to get to know yourself, because you will probably end up meeting the person you would never want to become. If you want to do something for yourself, start figuring out from what material your sweat is made of, start finding out from what material you are made of, find out who you are before you take the road to success, because the man you will become after you win will not be the same as the one you are now.

PAUL: What are you trying to say, that successes are often smarter than their owners?

SELF-CONFIDENCE: Yes, that's right. So don't let your own success teach you about who you are, because she will tell it the way she wants. Using her most effective magic tricks she will show you someone else, someone who can stand to be more radiant than you, someone who might not mind feeling less real as long as he can keep succeeding. *(Pause)* Tell me, have you ever considered how bright you can stand to be? Have you ever considered the possibility that your brilliance might decide to turn the enormous floodlights your ego uses to illuminate your achievements and try to blind you?

PAUL: Will you accept it as an answer if I tell you that often before an important decision I sit at the edge of my conscience and admire the rewards my pessimism is offering me to not even try?

SELF-CONFIDENCE: You should know that every question man hasn't found the courage to ask his sweat is a live grenade that insists on following him wherever he goes in his life.

PAUL: You should know that if you came today to ask me to pay back the emotional loans you gave my tears after my latest defeat, you chose the wrong day.

SELF-CONFIDENCE: I am impressed by your mind's inventiveness in terms of discovering arguments to convince you that it doesn't owe you anything anymore. If you look more carefully right in front of you, you will see your sorrow smiling at you from afar.

PAUL: I am warning you, I won't respect every bastard thought you are trying to give birth to right this moment in my mind.

SELF-CONFIDENCE: There you have the inadequacy of a mind that no longer respects its own whiteness. There you have it, so enjoy it!

PAUL: Will you let me, damn you, construct my next reality from materials I have chosen myself?

SELF-CONFIDENCE: No, I won't, but I'll let your reality construct you anyway that suits you best. Don't forget that man is created by the mistakes he has avoided making.

PAUL: Maybe even by the mistakes he has not made yet. I don't think my ego will be able to stand that. Who the hell sent before me today the only black cloud in the sky that would like to be even blacker, the only one that is proud of the storms it is going to use to dispense more misery to the people who will find themselves under it in the next few hours?

SELF-CONFIDENCE: If you want to know, I was sent by the parts of your soul you are running to hide from.

PAUL: Will you please let all the azure that still chooses to live inside me come find me to embrace me? I really need it so much. Stop hounding all my joys that demand of me to become part of my sorrow before they start explaining to me how to be happy.

SELF-CONFIDENCE: Don't talk about me, you are the one who is scared of the smartest fear your laughter hides inside it, not me.

PAUL: So, what are you trying to tell me, that defeatism is the ugliness of a soul?

SELF-CONFIDENCE: I am trying to tell you that the next happy moment in your life has arrived without you noticing and is sitting ten inches behind your back, intending to soon ask you to lower your head so it can whisper to you the worst question it can think of.

PAUL: What...

SELF-CONFIDENCE: If you are not emotionally armed, if you're not ready, I advise you to not turn around.

PAUL: I won't, I certainly won't. Tell me, is it carrying all my stainless steel memories with it or has it come alone?

SELF-CONFIDENCE: Yes it is, and it's the kind of memories that you will soon ask to grab you by the hand and start interpreting you.

PAUL: Please, leave me alone for a while, let me enjoy the few moments during the day that my soul has my ego's permission to dream.

SELF-CONFIDENCE: Poor man, I think I will let you enjoy for a bit those few moments during the day when your sorrow has your reality's permission to be cheerful.

PAUL: My sorrows' self-awareness just asked my permission to go to sleep, if you don't need it any longer.

SELF-CONFIDENCE: No, I don't… Have you ever wondered why your self-awareness' pockets were born full of holes?

PAUL: They are not holes, those are their back doors, dummy! Every self-awareness has at least one back door, to be able to whisk away all that she cannot understand.

SELF-CONFIDENCE: Come on now! You know that every completely corroded thought that lives in your mind wants to conceal inside it the most stainless steel truth you have.

PAUL: If you knew how much energy I have spent in my life to avoid having that thought! If you only knew how hard I am trying to constantly hide from what I am in danger of trans-

17

forming myself into in the next minute of my life, if in the end I don't hold out and I'm forced to admit what I am! What a huge struggle, what a difficult fight! If you only knew how big a piece of my ambiguity I throw every morning in the face of the breaking dawn so that it will let me live another day without having to understand all that it is trying to tell me!

SELF-CONFIDENCE: Wow, I'm impressed. I'm impressed by how big a part of your life you are able to hide in that spot of your fist you can only see when you don't know how to be aggressive, when you don't feel the need to demolish everything you find before you.

PAUL: You mean only when I don't need my fist?

SELF-CONFIDENCE: Yes I do.

PAUL: You should see then how big a piece of my insecurity I hide inside her!

SELF-CONFIDENCE: Every fist is an insecurity that hasn't found the way yet to express the pain her owner hides inside himself.

PAUL: How nice would it be if insecurities knew how to embrace, not only how to offend.

SELF-CONFIDENCE: If they did they would be called securities.

PAUL: Perhaps, perhaps…Every bullet is a pain that doesn't know how to suffer.

SELF-CONFIDENCE: I would say that every hatred is a pain that never learned how to look its owner's truth in the eyes. Tell me, have you ever asked your pain what it expects from you?

PAUL: Come on, stop with this pain, I can't stand it any longer; ask me something else please.

SELF-CONFIDENCE: Okay, have you ever asked your life's next step what it expects from you?

PAUL: Why should I? I am already anxious as it is about the future, I don't need to push it.

SELF-CONFIDENCE: So, what do you do, you just grab the first lifejacket you find before you, wrap it around your body and then go out the front door of your house and sit on the ground cross-legged, waiting for the rains to come?

PAUL: Please, don't dive into my mind to grab any bored sorrow of mine that doesn't know what to do with her life, so you can take her out and expect her to entertain you. They are probably right when they say that the starting line of a conscience coincides with the finish line of an ambiguity.

SELF-CONFIDENCE: You should stop living a life that wants at the same time to be somewhat less than white and something more that black.

PAUL: Maybe a life that seeks to be a different color than these two. Isn't this, though, the correctness of a conscience that realizes she may be wrong?

SELF-CONFIDENCE: If you keep on thinking like that, the part of the sky that doesn't know how to be blue anymore might come and hover right above you.

PAUL: I hope so…

SELF-CONFIDENCE: If I were in your shoes I would try to locate the part of the sky the clouds have not yet convinced to allow them to get on it and are sitting just outside pressed against each other waiting impatiently.

PAUL: Why do you say that? You know that you too have seen the effectiveness of my ambiguity when she fastens an iron ball to my feet every morning before I go to the office, so I won't be able during the day to get away from what I hope for.

SELF-CONFIDENCE: Hell, did you leave the interpretation of your life unlocked again?

PAUL: Why don't you try answering this question instead of me? Perhaps inside it you might find out in which period of your life you started hiding from me the pages of your operating manual which you've intentionally left blank. *(Pause)* Damn you, I always thought that you did it to make sure that my melancholy would try to squeeze inside them and write on their margins whatever she wanted, so I can read it forever.

SELF-CONFIDENCE: Come on, you are not even able to protect me from what your mind wants to do to me…

PAUL: Do me a favor, please. Try to interpret a teardrop of mine without insulting it. Come with me to help me catch in my mouth any silence that doesn't want to belong to me anymore so we can then start to sing it together, hoping that this might help you feel how far I am from understanding how strong my weakness is. Don't you see it? Across from you there is a man who can't even understand what the serenity he is already enjoying wants to tell him, unless he tries to find in every afternoon a scrawny, barely conscious full moon that's hiding in his character flaws, so it can help him realize what it is that he feels. It is this full moon that will later be afraid to go out all alone in the center of the sky, to avoid proving once again before all humanity how little of the glow it emits is actually its own.

How can such a brilliant entity be so weak? How can one of nature's most stunning creations be beautiful only when something else, the sun, decides to make it beautiful? What an amazing weakness this is, what a curse! What a great debt the poor thing must feel it is carrying on its back every day! What insecurity! *(Moved)* So this is my sister, the one I feel closer to than anyone else in my life. A weakness that is so perfect that in the end it seems to me even weaker, even more vulnerable. An explosively shiny entity that can light the whole universe, but doesn't even have the power of a single candle to illuminate itself without the sun's help. The largest mirror in the world… The saddest mirror in the world. That's how I feel, that's what I feel. So stop attacking my strength's authenticity, because I don't have that much left. There, that's all I have, and I guard it with my life so I won't lose it.

SELF-CONFIDENCE: Please don't let me build a silence from the most beautiful word I can think of right now, because I don't know what to tell you, how to answer you.

PAUL: My life is bereft of thought, bereft of beauty. Whatever is left from all that I cannot think about, whatever is left from the remnants of my mind, has already started spending all my intelligence just to become more attractive, leaving me to live embracing what is left when the beauty of my mind decides to throw off me the ugliness of my facade. I really like this freedom, I really do…

SELF-CONFIDENCE: Are you sure you can stand it?

PAUL: I am not sure, but I want to try.

SELF-CONFIDENCE: Let me help you. Give me a piece, the most courageous piece of the night that lives next to the most timid, the most faint-hearted darkness in your life, so I can see how I might eventually convince it to help you.

PAUL: I feel that my life is flooded with nights which appear to me dressed as fogs, nights that at any given time are ready to betray their darkness, since they know that the poor thing is always willing to give birth to its own end at the spot where man is able to hear for the first time all that his optimism has been shouting at him for hours. So I end up preferring the company of the gray from which the fog that does not have the ambition to have either a beginning or an end is made of, because I know that inside it lives the truth I did all I could to never believe in.

SELF-CONFIDENCE: It is this truth that begs you as soon as she's born to hammer in the middle of her body a nail made of the softest velvet.

PAUL: Self-confidence of mine, stand aside so I can pass. Sorrow of mine, I am coming, don't worry I won't be late.

SELF-CONFIDENCE: If you are going that way, let me give you a shield made of your toughest delusions, to protect you from the blows of your sorrow.

PAUL: Stocky silences, scrawny truths, who cares? My sorrow will squander them in no time, only to be able to convince me that I am not as repulsive as I seem. She pushes me to enter a room where I find dozens of disheveled truths, all thrown together, like in a tangled ball of yarn, each struggling with her own silence, to see which one will succeed in shaping my next melancholy the way she wants.

SELF-CONFIDENCE: Is she, perhaps, one of those truths which, when attacked by those words of yours that are born solely to offend and not to communicate, immediately rushes to defend your silence instead of you?

PAUL: I don't know. Let me continue.

SELF-CONFIDENCE: No, I won't let this much loved fairytale that's wandering in the unfathomable parts of your authenticity find those questions it doesn't know how to answer, not only to itself, but also to the parts of your logic that always doubted it. Hence, the secrets that your silence keeps from the first word waiting at the exit of your mouth for you to let it go complete its mission, become the loyal partners of your insecurity, the ones who right away will start constructing your next defeat on your behalf.

PAUL: I don't know…I'm not sure…

SELF-CONFIDENCE: Your truth is looking for a hero to believe in. Do you want to be your truth's hero?

PAUL: You know, every lie in my life keeps locked up inside it a word which, the first thing it wants to do as soon as it comes out of my mouth, is to turn around and try to grab me by the throat, and shake me violently until it manages to disentangle me from my sorrow. Dear God, how will I ever be able to become friend again with the part of my stupidity which out of all people refuses to talk to me?

SELF-CONFIDENCE: The personal traits of his which any man becomes familiar with when he sits for hours at his stupidity's exit, await you. Don't hesitate, go to them.

PAUL: And who told you that I can stand to be present during the conversation with my stupidity?

SELF-CONFIDENCE: But from whom can a man learn more things than his feature which knows him better than any other, the one to which he has bestowed the greatest strength so it can decide for him which next step in his life he should take?

PAUL: I know, you will tell me again not to believe that my stupidity is smarter than my intelligence.

SELF-CONFIDENCE: I will…

PAUL: And don't start telling me again how useful to me my character flaws might prove to be.

SELF-CONFIDENCE: I will tell you how much more likely than your intelligence your stupidity is to make you do whatever she wants. I will also tell you how much incredibly important information your shortcomings have been gathering about you for many years.

PAUL: How the hell do you explain the fact that while each time we have the same conversation I get so mentally tired, when we are done, for some reason that I don't know, I feel so relieved? It must be the inheritance my inadequacy leaves me to spend anyway I want in the future.

SELF-CONFIDENCE: It's the change your shortcomings will give you when you go to your honesty's cash register to try to buy them off your laziness.

PAUL: Stop offering me a new bouquet of beautiful injuries over and over. I can't stand it any longer. Leave me alone for a while, let me straddle, even for a few minutes, the breathlessness of the only sunbeam that wants to shine on me today more intensely than on any other person in the world and allow it to carry me to any spot of my life it chooses.

SELF-CONFIDENCE: It will take you to that spot of your life that believes less in you than any other.

PAUL: Let it take me there and let me grab from the edge of my private winter the two strongest deaths I will find, the ones that have been staring suspiciously at me for hours now, and go into the first florist shop my pessimism will find without the slightest help from me, stand in its middle and fall to my knees to apologize to every last flower in there.

SELF-CONFIDENCE: Why would you do that?

PAUL: Because the day before someone had cut them only so that people like me can spend a few hours watching the most beautiful death in the world, enjoy the beauty of nature slowly dying before my eyes, only to briefly infuse the ugliness of my world with a little beauty, hoping it will make it appear to be less ugly. How will I be able to reattach their little bodies, using as glue the dream they once had of being able to live forever in the place they were born without anyone pouncing on them to grab them and transform them into the beauty of their very death? You see, a flower doesn't die when it is cut, it dies the moment man puts it in a vase, making himself believe that he is making his life more beautiful this way.

SELF-CONFIDENCE: I can now clearly see in you the gift that the saddest day of winter left to your biggest guilt.

PAUL: What you see are the emotions last spring left at the front door of my heart, begging me to not ever try to understand them.

SELF-CONFIDENCE: I sense that today your life's darknesses will want to underline every mistake they find in the middle of your mind which, having nothing better to do, carefreely plays with the thoughts you have left at the edge of your reality.

PAUL: If you want to find out what I feel, find the first darkness that belongs more to me than to the night that is soon coming and ask it what it's hiding in its sides, because when I look at it, no matter the angle, I can't figure out what it's trying to hide from me.

SELF-CONFIDENCE: You mean its back sides?

PAUL: I didn't know it had more than one.

SELF-CONFIDENCE: You pessimism determines how many sides a darkness will have.

PAUL: And, possibly, how many I need as well...

SELF-CONFIDENCE: Perhaps...Anyway, you mean its back side?

PAUL: No, I mean the side I cannot see.

SELF-CONFIDENCE: I don't know.

PAUL: It's hiding the ambush which the solution to the biggest problem I am facing right now has set for me.

SELF-CONFIDENCE: Talking to you I feel as if a truth of yours has detached herself from the walls of your mind, grabbed me by the waist and is pushing me back and forth, trying to wedge me between the simplest and the most complicated emotion you are feeling right now.

PAUL: To determine which of the two she looks more alike?

SELF-CONFIDENCE: Probably.

PAUL: I don't know if you can see her, but right now my memory is tearing a piece off her body and is throwing it as far from me as she can, so that the next minute in my life won't be able to catch it and use it against me.

SELF-CONFIDENCE: I can't understand why you keep on trying to say what your mind is refusing to think for some time now.

PAUL: Sometimes I sense that my soul doesn't want to be more complicated than me. I have the impression that, if I ever let her be more ambitious than me, she would like to be able to give birth to much more valuable, more important emotions.

SELF-CONFIDENCE: How?

PAUL: In the fog you produce yourself, using as raw material any shortcoming of mine that can no longer talk to me because it doesn't know where to find me anymore, I stand upright, completely unable to see, but incredibly ready to feel. A few moments later, a young spring whose body brushes past mine, tries in vain, without looking, to cross my mind's highway, where my most defeatist thoughts rush by at infernal speed. It's these vulgar thoughts that always carry double headings inside them, perhaps double titles too, hiding between the second title's brackets whatever they didn't have the courage to say in the first one.

SELF-CONFIDENCE: The thoughts you speak of live right on the edge of your dignity and are able to bury their hands in the depths of your mind to try to grab any darkness that lives there to milk it, hoping they might extract from it the infinity you still haven't found a way to hide properly.

PAUL: What infinity are you talking about?

SELF-CONFIDENCE: The infinity that is very dangerous, because it exists in the midpoint of every happiness that doesn't know how to come close to you to try to find out if she wants to live with you. Besides, isn't that the definition of human misery, when the infinite and the minimal decide to live together in a soul? This way you end up like a miserable hermit wandering amid your most lavish darknesses, the ones that promise you convenience and comfort because they don't know how to offer you reality, stopping every so often at every oasis of light that is willing to exchange your mind's bankrupt charm with the emotional handouts you personally beg it for. Have you ever considered what you should do to buy a thought of yours, any thought of yours, off the reasons that make it want to make you feel miserable?

PAUL: What are you trying to hide in the back side of what you just said?

SELF-CONFIDENCE: Nothing, absolutely nothing. *(Pause)*

PAUL: How much more cruel than you must those cursed words be for you to intentionally leave them unspoken!

SELF-CONFIDENCE: Come on, you know there are no orphan silences.

PAUL: What do you mean?

SELF-CONFIDENCE: I mean that there is no unspoken word that doesn't know which emotion spawned it and, more importantly, the reason it spawned it.

PAUL: I feel that everytime our discussions reach the point where all your unspoken words start taking up all the space between us, ending up telling me much more than any other words you have uttered, my cowardice abruptly gets up and walks to the exit of my mind shrieking as loudly as she can, cursing and challenging my toughest words to come out and fight with her.

SELF-CONFIDENCE: When you discover how many Judases you have in your mind, all the Christs that live in those parts of your life you always considered insignificant will come find you.

PAUL: Please make me a ladder so I can climb up to the end of my soul and try to find where to start searching for who I am.

SELF-CONFIDENCE: You should know that the ladder you are asking for doesn't want to be made out of steps but out of hopes. Can you, though, grab onto them and climb it?

PAUL: I never knew how to answer the questions my own hopes asked me.

SELF-CONFIDENCE: Maybe because a thought that has never been hurt is usually more cruel than any other?

PAUL: Probably because there are people that don't know how to shape their future, using old rusted hopes that have been left unused for years.

SELF-CONFIDENCE: What do you mean?

PAUL: I mean the hopes that would rather stay forever in the past and never enter their owner's future.

SELF-CONFIDENCE: I get it. Are you asking me once again to spend hours bent over in your grayest private cloud to find the materials and help you build the step you need to climb? Again?

PAUL: Unless you prefer to dig in my future to unearth the thoughts buried by the questions my past has and can no longer stand letting them live inside it.

SELF-CONFIDENCE: You people are strange beings. First you attack us and hurt us with blows that don't stop unless they hear your cowardice calling them back to your normality, and then you bend over backwards to take care of us as best you can!

PAUL: That's not the way it is.

SELF-CONFIDENCE: I wonder what the hell you talk about with your stupidity when the two of you are left alone. Why do you insist on starting your day every morning by taking your first step from the spot where your shadow stopped the previous night? You know that an inch away from this spot live those wounds of yours that are permanently in love with your future and are constantly after you to persuade you to introduce them to it? How can you need me so much to survive and at the same time tirelessly breed inside you hundreds of my opponents? How can you fall at my feet begging me to help you and moments later start fighting me by deploying every last weakness of yours you have in your arsenal?

31

PAUL *(Shouting):* Can't you understand that I need my weakness more than I need my strength? Can't you understand that I am addicted to it much more than anything else in the world? Can't you understand that my weakness makes me feel much closer to what I am, vulnerable, sensitive, human? *(Erupting)* I need to feel, to feel – do you hear? Do you know how many times I got close to my logic and was afraid to touch her, lest she pass on to me the part of her strength I can no longer stand having inside me, the one that makes me so insufferable, so repulsive, shoving me hard and pushing me away from the people I love? Do you know how many times in my life I had to stop thinking to be able to go on living with my logic?

SELF-CONFIDENCE: What are you telling me now, that man might choose to suffer so he won't feel compelled to be happy?

PAUL: What I'm saying is that man often feels more comfortable when he is closer to his misery than to his happiness.

SELF-CONFIDENCE: It's amazing how good man is at using his mind to chase away the people he loves, while at the same falling at the feet of his soul to persuade her to go make them come back to him. I am sorry to say this, but your willingness to self-destruct is more ambitious than you.

PAUL: Perhaps it is. Perhaps it's even stronger than you. What should I do though? *(Pause)* Tell me, if I asked you to strip me of my self-destruction's determination, do you think you'd be able to do it?

SELF-CONFIDENCE: I am not in the habit of repairing broken dreams – especially the ones you yourself left for years exposed to the rain of your vanity to rust so much that they don't work anymore.

PAUL: It is dangerous to know how to repair something you don't know how to damage.

SELF-CONFIDENCE: Only if you don't need to remember all that you don't need to ever learn. *(Pause)* By God, I'm sure you wouldn't know what to do if tomorrow someone gave you ten new good qualities, and what's even worse, you would have no idea how to convince them to live in harmony inside you. I wonder, would you know how to use them?

PAUL: I would like to be able to convince my good qualities to stop fighting each other to see which one is stronger, but I can't. I think that if I managed to do it, I'd be less successful but much happier.

SELF-CONFIDENCE: I have the impression that because you are now unable to control the strength of your good qualities, you let the weakness of your shortcomings manage your life anyway it wants. Every day that goes by, you convince yourself that you weren't present at yet another defeat of your life in the past. This way you manage to destroy any proof of how good your shortcomings are at determining the quality of your life.

PAUL: Don't forget how demanding my ego is…

SELF-CONFIDENCE: To entertain your ego, every now and then you organize extravagant parades to honor the anniversaries of your great triumphs, mobilizing all your good qualities that can still give you the appearance of a veteran warrior who's still in fighting condition, while in fact you have become a lazy, pot-bellied bum. They parade before you while you sit in the golden chair given to you by the backup memory you use each time you don't want to stumble on what your main one can remember, holding by the hand all the questions that your vanity will never want to ask you.

PAUL: I can't hide it any longer. I am the product of the delusions that fabricate me when I can no longer fabricate my own truth. Or, if you prefer, I am the product of the imagination my incompetence uses to fabricate my delusions.

SELF-CONFIDENCE: Damn you, try making a sun out of the ten smallest truths you see when you look at your life from its darkest side. At least try… You don't need to reach today the part of your life which your normality never wanted you to find, but try though, take the first step.

PAUL: Yes, but I feel that in between each step of mine can fit emotions that are very dangerous because the damn things have managed to become almost invisible. Why don't you accept that there are souls which simply don't know how to read the slogans that the truth writes on those walls they have built to protect themselves from the decisions their owners' self-preservation has made?

SELF-CONFIDENCE: Why don't you send those street cleaning thoughts of your mind, the real heroes of your serenity that run around all day trying to clear your mind as quickly as they can from your own trash, before it realizes that it has thrown it out? This is the kind of trash that, once you get it out of your life and it lands on the ground, each piece instantly gives birth to a grenade which, if you don't find it fast enough, will manage to reach the center of your reality on its own and explode. (Pause) Anyway, are you no longer impressed by the fact that each time an important truth in your life comes to find you, it so happens that it is always just seconds after you've stopped crying?

PAUL: Come on. I am not even impressed by the fact that the fingermarks left behind in my mind by the words which any truth in my life I don't consider true enough leaves intentionally unspoken disappear in seconds! *(Pause)* Don't forget that for a man like me, who is not the biggest optimist there is, no matter how hard I try to compete with it, my past is always happier than me. Thus, every sunset I end up wrapping myself around the narrow spiral staircase that leads to my inadequacy –the emotion which probably cares for me more than any other in my life.

SELF-CONFIDENCE: You know, sometimes when you besiege the dreams the next step of your life has, you end up finding out what the previous one was made of.

PAUL: You don't have to prove to me how vast the dimensions of my chaos are. Trust me, I can feel on my own all that I no longer know how to understand. If you want to help me, do something to release me from the promise I made myself to never tell the whole truth to my lies again.

SELF-CONFIDENCE *(Sarcastically):* Oh, how becoming this invisible color your gaze just acquired is! If you want me to help you, let the fingers of your soul try to measure on me, without the slightest help from your logic, the safety distance you maintain from the various lies you use to make your life more likeable to your ego.

PAUL: You mean the lies I concoct to hide the death of a victory that doesn't know whom it defeated?

SELF-CONFIDENCE: I always thought that most victories are condemned to never know why they won. *(Pause)* How many times in your life have you felt that as soon as you won, your own victory turned around, focused her gaze on you and demanded to devour you?

PAUL: Please don't make me go so far back that I won't remember what I must do to go forward. I feel as if the first thought that comes to mind demands to place my next minute across from its own questions, across from anything emotionally illicit my mind can think of while it is doing everything it can not to think at all. I can't stand listening to the echoes that reverberate from its own cries for help, when it finds the courage to sit alone just a guilt away from the great truth it had borne itself and listen to what she has to confess.

SELF-CONFIDENCE: Ah, the weeping, the cries for help of a mind that does not know how to hurt is a weeping nobody can hear. Shredding its owner's self-awareness into a thousand pieces, the damn thing ends up causing unbearable pain.

PAUL: I can't bear listening to the echoes that come out of my mind when it starts calling by name all its biggest fears one by one as loud as it can.

SELF-CONFIDENCE: You know, though, that this happens when a sorrow's courage doesn't fit back in the bottle of ambiguity it came out of. Face it, the window through which you want to see what your life looks like when you are not present has chosen to keep its shutters closed most of the time.

PAUL: Well then, it seems that they're right when they say that self-confidences acquire truths from the realities they no longer consider their own.

SELF-CONFIDENCE: Okay, okay…

PAUL: How I wish I were one of those people who can with a single phrase, a single act -just one- remove entire darknesses from inside themselves! How I wish. How I envy them! Instead, everytime I lose a darkness, I immediately replace it inside me, putting one over the other, expanding daily the arsenal my sorrow will use to defeat me.

SELF-CONFIDENCE: At least you realize that the weapon your sorrow will use to defeat you is the darkness you have given her yourself. And please don't pretend you don't know that every morning, the reality that man throws in the trash as soon as he brushes his teeth has her way and sooner or later gets out of the sewers, in which the time he spends hoping to become more attractive has thrown everything it does not need to improve his own image, so she can hand him the bill for her services. There is no past that is satisfied knowing that it has only a single version of the future in it. There may not even be a past that agrees to have only one Judas in it.

PAUL: I don't know how to respond to you, I don't even know how to enter the next minute of my life without elbowing the previous one hard. I don't know how to convince my optimism to enter my next experience ahead of me, to make it less sharp for me, less able to cause me pain. The only thing I know is that the dreams I have about my past end up being much more useful to me than the dreams I have about my future. I see them coming from a distance, from the deepest part of my ambiguity, each holding in its right hand an unborn smile, and in its left an overly ambitious eraser.

SELF-CONFIDENCE: You know what this means? It means you have become the self-terminating product of the eraser your life uses to erase every happy moment from the next segment of your future you wish to enter.

PAUL: And here I thought I was the self- terminating product of my conscience's vanity!

SELF-CONFIDENCE: Today I don't want you to exceed the limits your most ambitious shortcoming has set for you. Today I don't want you to abuse what the end of your truth has promised to deliver to you.

PAUL: How the hell do you keep close to you a past that demands to have a different future than you?

SELF-CONFIDENCE: By letting your self-control pose any question it wants to the part of your past you do all you can to find out what it is hiding from you. Don't forget that as man grows older he learns how to avoid his past better. Trying not to irritate his self-confidence, he carefully hides in his past a key and a grenade. The key, to try to unlock the door to his self-awareness, and the grenade to blow it up, when disappointed he will realize that he will never find the courage to insert the key to open it. The less a man wants to know about his past, the happier he makes his favorite fog that's doing its best to hide from him his next step in life.

The more questions he insists on asking his past, the more transparent answers he gets from his future.

PAUL: Why?

SELF-CONFIDENCE: Because the future likes to respond to the questions you ask it not with words, but with deeds.

PAUL: I am so afraid of these damn questions, I really am. I see them constantly before me wherever I go. From the first minute each new sorrow of mine is born, they chase after me to convince me that the time has come for me to betray them, by cheating on them with my dignity. Everytime at the end, if I don't manage to give them an answer they like, they persuade my mind to throw itself in between the jaws of a vice, a huge red vice -red so that the blood my thoughts will soon spill won't show- and then they start tightening it until I stop thinking thoughts that are mine and start thinking thoughts I have borrowed from different realities than those I have experienced. Maybe this is the tool that was given to me as a gift when I turned eighteen by the last reality my adolescence ever used before she gave me a kick and sent me into my adulthood.

SELF-CONFIDENCE: If I am not mistaken, you once told me that a very odd looking reality had welcomed you into your adult life, giving you a strong slap and a sweet kiss at the same time. Was it the same one?

PAUL: No, no, not at all…

SELF-CONFIDENCE: In these questions live the equations your logic needs to solve to be able to adapt to the new dimensions your past acquires while walking at a constant distance of a guilt away, parallel to every new day of your life.

PAUL: This way I became the favorite stain my past leaves on the surface of every new day, once I finish washing off it the blood of the previous one.

SELF-CONFIDENCE: And you know, we self-confidences get all our strength from each of your pasts. The stains you refer to -any part of your past your truth has deliberately left undefined, any emotional clearing in your memory that contains even the smallest darkness that sneaked into her- end up digging into the ground beneath your own foundations, trying to weaken your self-confidence, by making you not believe in your own good qualities, your own strength anymore. It's not the future, the circumstances of his life, or the problems he faces, that open the door and let insecurities enter a man's mind, it's his own past.

PAUL: Ah, this struggle of humans with their past. What a fight that is!

SELF-CONFIDENCE: Don't you often feel that your past has with time become more capable than you?

PAUL: Almost all the time...

SELF-CONFIDENCE: It's not more capable, it simply knows you well, extremely well, probably better than you know yourself. You see, you often choose to forget whatever is not convenient to remember, whatever makes your next step into the future more uncertain, less stable. The damned past, though, never forgets anything. Your past is the cursed proof of who you are. In it you will find all your deeds, all your words. You can't escape it, because it would be like trying to escape your own body.

PAUL: There are times when I believe that my past is more mine than my own body, that it defines my life more than anything else. I know that the better I feel when I can stand to sit across from my past looking into its eyes, because that's the only way it wants me to look at it, the better I feel about my future. I realized a long time ago that often it's my past that takes me by the hand and places me in whichever minute of my next sorrow or my next happiness it wants.

SELF-CONFIDENCE: Exactly. Every new action of yours, every new word you utter, is added to the long parade of the preceding ones, which have formed a huge line, an endless shadow behind you and are following you day and night wherever you go.

PAUL: This is the world's heaviest shadow, a shadow that doesn't need light to survive, just new mistakes. It collects light from everything I do right and darkness from everything I do wrong, and gets re-energized everytime I don't have to remember who I am to be able to understand who I must become.

SELF-CONFIDENCE: Man cannot escape, cannot slip away from his future by fooling his past; he can only understand it, not by simply understanding what happened, but by realizing who he became during every action of his, every word he uttered. This is the only way he can remove the bullets from the gun his past is holding to his temple each time he feels unhappy without knowing why.

PAUL: So, what are you trying to say, that I am what my past allows me to be?

SELF-CONFIDENCE: You are the truth with which your past is rushing to clothe you, before you decide to go deep inside it to start trying to find out who you really are. You are the silence which your past uses to wrap around the next word you want to utter, when you don't know what favor to ask from the phrase you are about to say. Face it. Man's only ally each time something happens for the first time in his life is his own past. Within it he searches to find, as quickly as he can, similar circumstances to draw instant information on how to behave, knowledge on who he was, and so be able to understand who he should become. You see, your past knows a lot more than you, because, to save your conscience from the trampling of its unbearable shadow, you have given your crafty mind a standing order to endlessly run up and down your memories with its enormous eraser and remove whatever it thinks doesn't do you any good to remember.

PAUL: There is no other silence in the world that can pierce my ears and make me writhe in pain like the one I hear everytime I ask my past the questions I know it will refuse to answer.

SELF-CONFIDENCE: Your past is the only part of your life that refuses to discuss, let alone negotiate with you. Without giving you a chance to react, it instantly shoves in its pockets whatever happens in your life, every new word that comes out of your mouth, every new deed that comes out of your hands. The damn thing is a crafty gypsy that picks up everything and doesn't throw anything away. It keeps everything inside it and refuses to hand back or exchange with you even the smallest, most insignificant memory.

PAUL: That's why everytime you force me to make a U-turn in my life and fall at my past's feet to beg for a piece of it, any piece, so I can drag it to my present, hoping I might be able to disarm it, to take away from it all the cursed power it has to control me, I end up arguing with my truth which, standing right in front of me, ten inches from my face, is furiously screaming at me. How I wish I knew how to translate every word my past refuses to tell me to avoid wounding me into something I can understand!

SELF-CONFIDENCE: The silence that likes to live inside your past is the hardest silence in the world to learn how to decipher, when once in a while it decides to talk to you.

PAUL: Self-confidence of mine, I never could understand why my past enjoys so much making me unhappy. Will you tell me?

SELF-CONFIDENCE: It's not your past that makes you unhappy. It's everytime you come face to face with it and a few seconds later it takes out of its raincoat that hand mirror to which your eyes are instantly riveted, trying with great effort to draw out of it as much new information as possible about who you are. And as you know, it is this information that you throw at my face right after, so I will do with it what I can, find a way to use it as fuel so that your optimism can function again the way you want it to.

PAUL: You're right, the past is ultimately a man's mirror, a mirror that does its best to keep its surface as blurred as possible.

SELF-CONFIDENCE: No, no, it's not the mirror. It's the mirror's owner.

PAUL: What are you trying to say, that it won't let me look at my face's reflection whenever I feel like it?

SELF-CONFIDENCE: Exactly.

PAUL: So it's my past that determines if I will figure out who I am? Why do I allow it to have so much power? Why do I let it dominate me in such a humiliating way?

SELF-CONFIDENCE: I hear what you are saying and I feel like laughing. It's as if you believe that your past is intelligent and reveals or hides from you whatever it wants, as if it's in a mood to play games with you. Don't you realize that your past is such a capable opponent of your happiness, your serenity, not because it is terribly clever, but because it is utterly dumb? It does not think, therefore it cannot negotiate. It does not speak to you, so you cannot, as usual, mobilize your best arguments to persuade it to do what you want. Your past is nothing more than a huge data bank containing all your actions and all your words, a non-negotiable entity, a massive mountain whose peak is not in the sky but in the abyss. You don't need to climb it to conquer it, you need to descend to the lowest basements of yourself till you reach its peak, which is located inside you, in your deepest part.
The formidable force your past exerts over you is me. Each time you seek my help is as if you are asking me to show you from scratch how strong you are, managing with the magic tricks you want me to perform to hide all your weaknesses one by one behind the illicit gazes you throw at you self-worth. Don't you understand that your strength is in your very past? Man is victorious in the future because he can stand to not lower his gaze when his past is staring at him with that overpowering, stern look -a look that hides

inside it an infinity capable of wrapping itself around and instantly choking to death even the strongest intellect! You often enter your future as the front passenger in the car your past is driving, not because you can't drive, but because you feel much safer when you let it drive you.

PAUL: Ah, those ambiguous full stops my past likes to place at any point in my future it wants! By God, I think I will come out of our conversation mentally traumatized but much stronger. Self-confidence of mine, are the tools of my meager logic good enough for me to be a happy man? Are they enough? Please tell me, tell me, because tonight I am depending on you more than any other time in my life, not because I must make an important decision in the next few minutes, but because I feel the need to finally understand what my happiness wants from me. You poor thing, how many times have I sent you to the most unpredictable part of the battles I fought in my life so you could bring my happiness back to me safe and sound!

SELF-CONFIDENCE: You do know, though, that the definition of misery is the happiness that doesn't know how to believe in herself, doesn't know how not to be ashamed of how happy she really is?

PAUL: What will be left of my life, I wonder, if I eliminate the reasons that make me feel happy?

SELF-CONFIDENCE: The reasons that make you feel that you are the most precious ornament of your own lies. This is the way delusions choose to masquerade as uninterpreted miracles and nights as expendable promises, promises which no longer feel obliged to do what they promised.

PAUL: During these very moments I sense the emotional pirates that live inside me wanting to abduct me away from my own happiness.

SELF-CONFIDENCE: Will you permit me to turn the page on your argument and let you introduce yourself anew to the side of your truth that always despised you?

PAUL: You crafty devil you, are you really so ambitious that you think you can extract with one deft move all the unprocessed centuries of sorrow that insist on living in my head?

SELF-CONFIDENCE: No, I only want to persuade you to take in hand, one by one, all the locks in your life that you have personally constructed using the strongest steel and strip them of the power each one has acquired over time, namely to be able with this one move you mentioned to hold you captive in their own secrets.

PAUL *(Raises his hands up high):* Courage of mine where are you? I really need you so much right now. I can't stand being the biggest fan of my cowardice, left all alone in the vast arena following my great defeat, to celebrate wildly. I can't stand being the best customer of my own rage, waiting in the long line formed in the middle of the night by a thousand sorrows of mine for my rage's store to open its doors, so I can finally buy her latest model. Courage of mine, help me find a way to defend myself from the merciless attacks of my own memories, as they are poised to punch me with the fists I made for them myself, until they smash every last optimism inside me into a thousand pieces.

SELF-CONFIDENCE: What makes you believe that you are the sole owner of the questions you are afraid to ask your own life?

PAUL: *(Continuing)* I see my past holding in one hand the defeats that are still in love with me and in the other a huge broom with which it chases after me to erase the tracks of the long walks I took inside my conscience while trying to find out what I'm made of.

SELF-CONFIDENCE: So long as you plant questions in the soil you tread on, tomorrow will keep refusing to tell you what it thinks of you. The longer you keep loading new questions on the wings you use to free yourself from the answers you don't want your soul to give you, the fewer the chances that you will be able to fly away, to escape the mental quagmire you don't know how to persuade yourself to stop producing.

PAUL: Sometimes I feel as if in the middle of my mind there lives a beautiful old lady that holds a pink basket in her left hand and hands out free long, sharp, stainless-steel thorns to every thought of mine that passes before her, to give it the ability to pierce the sides of every happy moment that awaits me just behind my ambiguity to experience it.

SELF-CONFIDENCE: I see that you have managed to convince the sun to not dispense his beams today for free.

PAUL: Why, do you think that my sorrow intends to hand out my tears today for free? *(Pause)* Either way, how many sunbeams do you think can fit in a soul that can no longer feel joy because she has temporarily lost the ability to fully comprehend what the sun allows her to see?

SELF-CONFIDENCE: It depends on what you see when you look your next decision in the eyes…

PAUL: The things I see in my self-control's store display which I would never want to buy.

SELF-CONFIDENCE: Don't try to be your sorrow's favorite messenger. It doesn't suit you. Stop letting your feelings of guilt shape your dreams the way they want.

PAUL: Damn life, as it turns out, your tallest, most impenetrable walls are actually completely invisible!

SELF-CONFIDENCE: Don't let your mind build doors between you and your next happiness.

PAUL: Not only does it build them, but it seems to me that once it finishes each one, it immediately starts nailing it up, using, instead of nails, those drops of my sweat that never wanted to perspire. It wants to really make sure that I will never be able, no matter how hard I try, to convince them to open them for me.

SELF-CONFIDENCE: There's what you can learn today from your cowardice.

PAUL: What?

SELF-CONFIDENCE: That your mind won't need you anymore today.

PAUL: Please, today don't let the sea of my truth wash up hundreds of underage fires on the only beach that my mind still has access to.

SELF-CONFIDENCE: What happened? Doesn't your mind have any other bridges for you to get across? *(Pause)* Ssh…Stop talking for a while and listen to what the darkness that is ready to be born a few feet away from you has been whispering to you for a few minutes now.

PAUL *(Interrupting):* I know, I know. You never leave me, anyway, without reminding me; darknesses are born when a man's optimism decides for the first time to take a step back. *(Long pause)* While we've been talking, I have been leafing through the reasons I should not be sad, and I just came across a page that is blank. Why do you think that is?

SELF-CONFIDENCE: I don't know, but it's possible that inside it live those words of yours which, since they know that they're not part of your future, have turned around and are rushing to flood your past. As soon as they were born, they placed their dignity above their comfort and chose by themselves to not speak.

PAUL: I really get so confused whenever I see my soul not feel obliged to explain to me what this thing that I feel actually means.

SELF-CONFIDENCE: Don't be so sure that the entry of a happiness is the exit of a sorrow.

PAUL: I am not even sure about that anymore. But even if I were, I would have every reason to doubt after being mercilessly chased all these years by the footnotes my happiness writes down each time she sees me happy without there being a single reason my logic would consider important. Those damn footnotes are chasing after me to prove to me that the happiness I see in the store display where my conscience is showcasing all the products she is willing to sell to me, is not the same as the happiness I will experience if I can stand to not buy anything from her.

SELF-CONFIDENCE: You really like to dance barefoot on the broken glass that your ambiguity has been throwing wherever you intend to step, while you don't stop looking provocatively into my eyes. It's impressive how, while you struggle tooth and nail not to show the least annoyance, at the end of the dance you have managed to fill your entire life with pain, to such an extent that you can't stand it anymore and you fall down a few feet before you reach that long black table located at the emotionally steepest edge of your life.

PAUL: Oh, are you talking about the table that has moved to the spot in my life where I can only bear to stand upright?

SELF-CONFIDENCE: Exactly. So, there you will be forced to sit and after catching your breath, you will begin to slowly drink your sorrow along with all the zeros your self-criticism wouldn't stop shoving in your pocket all day, each time I turned my eyes elsewhere.

PAUL: Let me ask you something, do you believe I deserve my self-criticism?

SELF-CONFIDENCE: I don't know, but I am sure that you deserve the melancholy it causes you to feel.

PAUL: Why?

SELF-CONFIDENCE: Because you still haven't found a way to deserve your happiness.

PAUL: Do you know that the opinion I have of myself often leads me to a path barely wide enough to be simultaneously crossed by a conscience and the biggest mistake she has ever made herself on my behalf?

SELF-CONFIDENCE: I am impressed by that. How fast do you think you can produce a brand new sorrow from completely different materials than the previous one?

PAUL: You should see how fast I can produce a sorrow using parts of myself that don't even recognize each other.

SELF-CONFIDENCE: Please don't raise the bar I must leap over to make you happy.

PAUL: Come, let me help you out a bit. Do you know which distance a teardrop will never be able to measure, no matter how hard it tries?

SELF-CONFIDENCE: No.

PAUL: The distance between two truths.

SELF-CONFIDENCE: I think it's time you took out of you those firefighting thoughts you have and put out the fire you yourself are ready to set in the next few seconds in the part of your brain you can rarely access.

PAUL: Do nails exist, I wonder, that, no matter how hard man hits on them, refuse to pierce?

SELF-CONFIDENCE: Yes they do, the same way there are sorrows that have decided to never hurt anyone again.

PAUL: I've never met any of them.

SELF-CONFIDENCE: You know, vases don't give birth to flowers, they just help them die. Today though, a vase has decided for the first time in its life to lie. To any passerby who comments on the beautiful flowers it has in it, it replies that it gave birth to them. Today is the day it believes so little in itself that it is willing to shape the truth anyway it wants. It forgets that the only thing it knows how to do is to delay for a couple of days the death of the flowers it contains, constantly offering them false hopes that it will soon discover a way to prolong their life. So, you should try to figure out the difference between water and soil in your own life, to understand for how long you can keep a happiness alive once you cut her off the soul that gave birth to it.

PAUL: Are you trying to say that…

SELF-CONFIDENCE: All I am trying to say is that you must embrace your humility again, the soil in your life which you consider ugly and unimportant.

PAUL: What makes you think that white has fewer dreams than all the other colors?

SELF-CONFIDENCE: You know, a half-open door has more questions than a closed one.

PAUL: And more misgivings too. Please tell your words to stop spreading these treacherous, invisible fogs all over my mind. I already have enough, I don't need any more.

SELF-CONFIDENCE: You are lucky they don't plant those fogs that smile at you as soon as you look at them, and at the same time politely show you the wrong way to go…

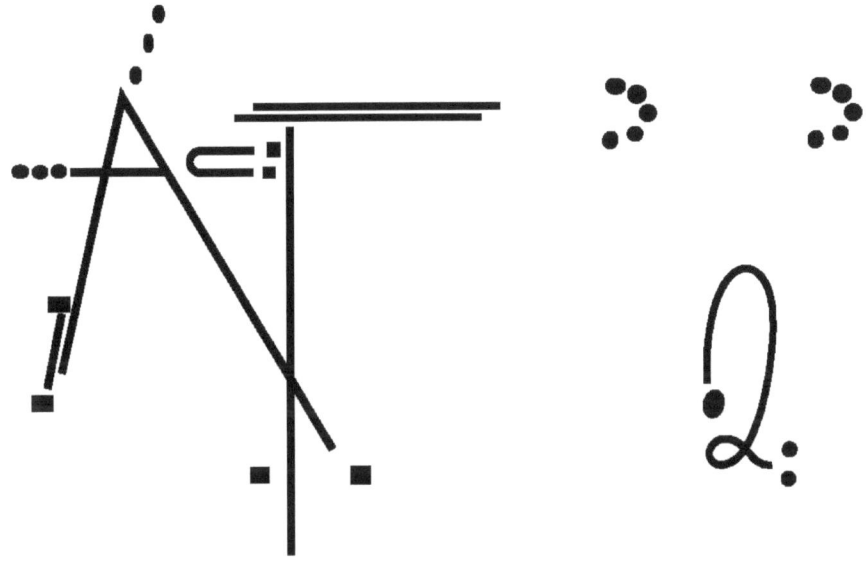

SELF-CONFIDENCE: What more do you want from me anyway? You always keep asking me for something. Don't you understand? I don't have the answers to all your questions –the answers have me. They keep me caged in the insecurity of having to explain to you things I don't understand, concepts which no matter how hard I try, I cannot grasp. You are being so unfair to me! You keep me imprisoned in the deepest dungeons of your truth and at the same time let me loose, free to wander in any part of your lies I wish. What I wouldn't give to see them both silenced!

PAUL: And you, why do you tie me to my own good qualities, preventing them from helping me define what makes me happy even when I don't end up winning? Whenever I spend time talking to my individuality, you jump up and remind me that it's time I discovered how alike I am with the pieces of my courage that admire my mediocrity more than they admire me. You insist on hosting my biggest doubts inside you, just so you can make me run like a schoolchild on its way to find the person it hates more than any other in life to confide to him the part of his character that makes him at the same time different but also sad, to help him understand it, to make it his and thus save him from it.

Everytime I talk to you I see my life's trash keeping notes a few feet away. Where are you when I need you? You often abandon me all alone to duel with my mediocrity until she convinces me of how mediocre I really am. Where are you during the tough times, when my mind decides to allow every last pleasure it feels to run with the various free falls of my life, so they can all join forces and start wrestling against me? Why do you humiliate me by leaving me defenseless, making me seem to the people around me as nothing more than your meager gratuity? This is what I have ended up becoming. My self-confidence's gratuity! So admire me, admire me! I feel as if you have put a collar and leash on me, the way they used to do long ago with wild animals, and have taken me out on walks through my life to embarrass me, forcing me to do stupid tricks in front of everyone, using as assistants any of my good qualities that can still stand to live with me!

SELF-CONFIDENCE: You make me feel more powerful than I actually am...

PAUL: You are my Trojan horse, the one which I now permanently breed inside me, an insidious creature that forever lives in the fortress it was sent to capture, a winter made of all the disappointed days a life can pick out of the leftovers a conscience leaves behind when she decides to devour her owner's joy. You know me so well that, before I even get a chance to learn how to manage every newborn guilt of mine, you have already managed to unlock it from its future obligations, so it can freely move among all the parts of my soul I have left completely defenseless. To every triumph of mine you demand, before it even finishes enjoying its victory, to add the footnotes that you want, and for every one of my defeats you demand to remove from my mind the excuse for being defeated. Leave me alone, I no longer want you to force me every evening to measure the dimensions of the fog I constructed during the day, so that I won't be able to realize what actually happened to me. I don't want you to, I really don't...

SELF-CONFIDENCE: Every man's cowardice is the legacy left every evening on his nightstand by the person he became during the day that just ended.

PAUL: Don't throw in my face what I'm asked by the usual answers I give you everytime I don't know how to find a new method to lose my way in my own life.

SELF-CONFIDENCE: I really enjoy seeing you wrestle with the effigy of yourself which the day that just ended gave you as a gift!

PAUL: Why, do you happen to have any quantity of consumable yesterday you can spare?

SELF-CONFIDENCE: No I don't, but I can offer you for free some half-wrecked ghosts left behind by one of your thoughts that decided to leave your mind forever before you finished thinking it.

PAUL: Please stop messing with my past and turn your head to tomorrow.

SELF-CONFIDENCE: A quick excavation of your cowardice probably wouldn't take long to bring to light the flavor that tomorrow would like to have.

PAUL: Excavation, for what reason? To find what? Everything that knows me better than I know it? To find that growing up I discovered that my lie was growing faster than me and, without asking me, slowly became the measure of my success, turning my lips into the heavy, sophisticated weapons I used to kill any trace of courage that remained in the small bit of kindness that could still stand to live in my truth? To discover what? That, embracing all the wounds I could fit in my pessimism, I always ended up, a minute before I stepped through the door of my personal insecurities to go to work, throwing them one after another at my conscience's face, which for yet another morning looked at me terrified, wondering what I was going to do to her in the next few hours? This way, I went so far as diving into the torrent of the interpretation of my life, to try to save the effigy of who I would like to become during the day from drowning, while it was trying as hard as it could to save what I already am.

SELF-CONFIDENCE: Are you talking about the torrent that, instead of water, is made of hundreds of words, which you are ready at any time to utter, without knowing exactly what you want to say?

PAUL: Yes, the one whose course is full of the sharpest stones belonging to my conscience, stones that stand proud, steadfast in the middle of its most hazardous bends, waiting for my body to smash into them so they can wound it as much as they can.

SELF-CONFIDENCE: How strange you must feel knowing that it is you that put them there!

PAUL: The strangest thing is that while I'm struggling to survive amid the raging fury of my own words, the ones I see tumbling down from the sky wrapped at the end of each sunbeam are red drops, each one holding on tightly to its own explanation for my unhappiness.

SELF-CONFIDENCE: An explanation that each red drop is coming to deliver to you personally?

PAUL: Obviously.

SELF-CONFIDENCE: You have made yourself feel as if you are the permanent captive of the confidence your mediocrity gives you when she keeps you imprisoned at that magic spot in your life where your victories don't dare to go.

PAUL: How I wish I could spend some time with them so they could explain what they want from me!

SELF-CONFIDENCE: You live permanently tied to the part of yourself that always wanted to stay as far away from you as possible, the part that always sought to be less unhappy than you wanted to be, tied to every teardrop of your intelligence borne on your behalf by those victories of yours that come from the past to help you realize what you could have been if you had not chosen to live constantly on your knees instead of standing up. Every morning I see you next to me, getting up to go to work, starting your day by apologizing for all that you ever wanted but ultimately will never manage to accomplish. Your own self-awareness, as soon as she senses that you are looking to find pieces of yourself in the emotional trash you threw out last night, makes a running start and falls between you and your mind, trying to protect you from the questions your optimism still has, because she knows that right in those moments they can only hurt you.

PAUL: Why do I feel that if I look into your eyes for long, I will be able to see through the image reflected in them who I will be tomorrow?

SELF-CONFIDENCE: Because the only part of your mind that can translate your mediocrity into happiness belongs to me.

PAUL: I feel that the part of midnight that refuses to live anywhere else in my life except within you, is using me so it can live a few more hours, hoping it might get a chance to see daylight.

SELF-CONFIDENCE: Do you want to talk to me about the part of your past that no longer wants to have the same future as you?

PAUL: I see that you often try to become the enemy of the answers you owe to yourself.

SELF-CONFIDENCE *(Interrupting):* You mean those questions your future is afraid to ask you? *(Pause)* Now I understand why they say that egos see better in the dark!

PAUL: Why should a mind not be able to distinguish an ego from the darkness in the middle of the night?

SELF-CONFIDENCE: Because truths discover their own stupidity at night.

PAUL: You're right. After all, I often need your help to understand what my guilt has decided to tell me.

SELF-CONFIDENCE: Have you ever wondered in which part of your life darkness prefers to blossom?

PAUL: You've asked me this before... In the old days I really didn't know. And if I did, do you think I could see it? *(Pause)* Maybe in the spot that can't be reached by the most optimistic ray my heart sends while trying to touch the world around her, hoping she might understand it?

SELF-CONFIDENCE: No, no. It's where your sorrow starts doubting her own strength. Don't forget that the heart's back door never learns how to hide from the front one.

PAUL: Indeed. Besides, from her I learned how to take back my scream –the one she had lent my mistakes so they can better express what they feel.

SELF-CONFIDENCE: What will you do with the ludicrously small tip your ego will soon throw at the face of tomorrow?

PAUL: It doesn't matter, because I have long stopped believing that I am smarter than the man I will be tomorrow.

SELF-CONFIDENCE: If you want to understand, let your mind free to get out from inside you and go lie down between the smartest zero, which your luck has been trying for days to give you for free, and the part of your truth that no longer believes that it's so true anymore.

PAUL: I've done this before and after a while I ended up trying to separate the different abysses inside me, which suddenly began to fight with each other without any reason.

SELF-CONFIDENCE: How much longer will you carry in your back pocket the check your reality wrote to you so you will keep your mouth shut?

PAUL: Maybe now is not the time to confess that next to my other self I discovered a third one?

SELF-CONFIDENCE: What made you believe that my inventiveness would be so unambitious that it would let you have only two selves?

PAUL: It really bothers me that I let my self-confidence determine how many selves I can have!

SELF-CONFIDENCE: You know that you're the one who granted me this right.

PAUL: How? When?

SELF-CONFIDENCE: When you didn't respect your first self.

PAUL: Dear God, what is the right viewpoint for a mind that no longer wants to see? Self-confidence of mine, can you please help me find a way to regret everything I never found the courage to accomplish?

SELF-CONFIDENCE: Are you talking about the kind of joy that likes to hide in the sadnesses that don't know why they are sad anymore?

PAUL: Yes, they are the sorrows which, long after you open their door, you start realizing why you should never have tried to get in them.

SELF-CONFIDENCE: Come on, you know there are doors that are made to never open.

PAUL: As there are autumns that refuse to be born, to become part of your life, part of your time, taking a step back and shoving you hard so you are forced to go straight into winter. And you know that damn winter won't let you take even a single August day with you, so it can trick you, giving you hope that summer might come back one day soon. Will you please let me get drunk by drinking the last hope that August day's optimism contains?

SELF-CONFIDENCE: Before you get drunk on your defeatism, let the first day of spring confide to you what for months now it didn't know how to tell you.

PAUL: I will do that…

SELF-CONFIDENCE: Speaking of doors, you always were one of those people who find the door to their melancholy almost always open.

PAUL: Yes, my melancholy has become the pimp of my life's next minute. You see, my shortcomings really insist on wanting to know how far the fingertips of my most hopeful optimism can reach.

SELF-CONFIDENCE: Isn't it time for you to admit that you belong to your back side?

PAUL: I won't answer you, because if I do, I will upset the parts of my strength that still speak to me. Please let me preserve my good relationship with them. You see, I really need them!

SELF-CONFIDENCE: What will you tell your cowardice, though, when she asks you to explain what you are scared of?

PAUL *(Interrupting her):* That I'm scared of becoming the man on whose lips only smiles that insist on being invisible will come to visit from now on. I know, I know.

SELF-CONFIDENCE: Just as well …

PAUL: My dam sadness is the only part of myself that wouldn't prefer to be something else. Please teach me how to hear the secrets my sadness whispers to every next hour of my life.

SELF-CONFIDENCE: Stop making love to tomorrow, thinking that you don't cheat on yesterday.

PAUL: My sorrow has already started concocting a different kind of relief in a part of my heart which for years has been living outside my body. Her flavor is ready to buy me from my next minute. *(Pause)* I really need to believe in a tomorrow that trusts my strength more than it trusts the strength of my past.

SELF-CONFIDENCE: As long as you don't confuse your reality's emergency exit with the entrance to your next hope, you will be okay. Beware of tomorrow, beware of it. It has this uncanny ability to cover with rust in just seconds whatever you intend to touch, to prevent you from tasting the joy, the liveliness it has in it.

PAUL: Tell me, is there an impasse in a man's life that wants to be more optimistic than him? Because each one I've seen so far tries to be more defeatist than any other. Before you reply, let me spread my emotional armor on the table so I can see which parts of it your words will try to pierce.

SELF-CONFIDENCE: Still, you have to admit that there is a part of your life where even your most gigantic "no" conceals an odd kind of optimism inside it.

PAUL: So what do you advise me, to start producing smiles from now on out of those old sunbeams I have tucked away in the deepest drawers of my pessimism?

SELF-CONFIDENCE: The most important magic trick one can learn on his own is how to hide from himself as quickly as possible.

PAUL: You mean to hide from his own truth?

SELF-CONFIDENCE: No, I don't.

PAUL: Do you mean the truth he tells his lies so they will stop bothering him?

SELF-CONFIDENCE: No, I mean to hide from what actually happened in his life, so he won't have to often come into contact with the person he swore he would become on the last day of his adolescence.

PAUL: How come I've become so good at hiding my defeats behind the statues I put up in honor of my triumphs?

SELF-CONFIDENCE: Because you are much better at being miserable that you are at being happy. Anyway, you don't hide them behind them but inside them, and not even there, since you simply use your defeats to make the pedestals for the statues you want to put up to honor your triumphs.

PAUL: I want to hold hands with all my defeats, the ones I never admitted that I managed to produce by myself without the slightest help from anyone else. I want us to sit for hours all around in a circle and toss in the middle all the unspoken words, the ones that, because I never found the courage in me to utter them, insist on making every minute I experience unbearable, and set them on fire so I can see what is left in a life that finally dares to kiss her cowardice on the mouth. Thus, in the company of my defeats, we will all reach out with our hands to touch each other's wounds.

SELF-CONFIDENCE: Inside every defeat, if you can show her the respect she deserves, you will find an old smile of yours waiting for you, one of those you personally betrayed so you won't have to ever explain it to your happiness.

PAUL: Are you telling me that I must rip out the malfunctioning miracle hidden inside every defeat of mine so I can give it to my arrogance to swallow before I even get a chance to get to know it? *(Pause)* If everytime I smiled I had to explain to my happiness the reasons I smiled…

SELF-CONFIDENCE: I am telling you that man is a product of his defeats. Every defeat has much to offer him, if he shows her the respect he owes her. A man's defeats are the mentor who will show him who he really is –simply by setting the very same mirror he uses daily at an angle from which he has never seen himself before, an angle only his great defeats know how to find. This angle instantly neutralizes all the phony gimmicks he uses to cover, to hide his true worth from his own fears. You see, only great defeats can make a person see through the extravagant clothing he has put on the lie he himself has become, so he can satisfy the version of his truth which, no matter how hard she tries each time he stands naked before her, cannot explain to him what it is that she sees.

PAUL: I can't remember where I put those days that refuse to hold in them anything else except breathtaking sunsets.

SELF-CONFIDENCE: Do you mean those truths that like to carry with them, wherever they go, all the overweight asterisks in your life, whose weight you cannot bear to carry on your own any longer?

PAUL: The way you are going, you will force me to get back into bed with those questions of mine that can survive only outside my head.

SELF-CONFIDENCE: Find inside you any character trait of yours that is made of soil and truth, find it and start confessing to it all the favors your arrogance was asking from you all these years.

PAUL: I should probably confess to it what I've been trying to do to it all these years.

SELF-CONFIDENCE: Can you feel your lies, which for hours now have been circling over your head trying to pick the next yesterday they like best out of the ones that live inside you? See if you can, by stretching out your arm and hugging your silence, learn how to listen to the whispers of the words which, because in your teens you didn't consider them especially worthwhile, you ended up inadvertently losing and since then you have never been able to find them again.

PAUL: Are you telling me that they have come today to find me?

SELF-CONFIDENCE: Perhaps, perhaps…

PAUL: Do you think I should not try to write the last chapter of my personal myth before I start believing in my truth?

SELF-CONFIDENCE: As long as you pray, you believe.

PAUL: As long as you walk, you may fall.

SELF-CONFIDENCE: As long as you create, you are being created.

PAUL: As long as you please, you are pleased.

SELF-CONFIDENCE: Can you, however, still recognize the emotional materials you used to construct yourself?

PAUL: Not all of them… *(Pause)* Now that I think about it, only the ones that owe their presence to my unhappiness.

SELF-CONFIDENCE: I could never understand why you always liked to cheat on yourself with your misery.

PAUL: Not always, only when I couldn't understand why I failed to answer a single question out of those my happiness asked me. *(Pause)* Why, do you doubt that if you dig for hours deep inside you, you will find in your smile, inside any of your smiles, a teardrop that is running as fast as it can, to have time to hide as far as possible from your sorrow?

SELF-CONFIDENCE: Don't forget that I still owe you those two miseries I had promised you one night.

PAUL: Will you please let me lie down for a while between my free fall and the first teardrop which, seeing it run down my skin, I won't be able to recognize as my own?

SELF-CONFIDENCE: So you want me to let you grab the light that demands to hide in it the kind of darkness that believes more in the day than in the night?

PAUL: Yes, I do. If you don't let me, I have the impression that midnight will choose in the next few minutes to intentionally shipwreck itself three feet away from my serenity, which has been waiting for hours to meet me. Poor midnight won't be able to reach her to unload from its holds all those pieces of my sadness I was never able to understand why they insisted on making me sad all these years. Can't you see? My mind has no more handholds I can hang on to so I won't fall down!

SELF-CONFIDENCE *(Interrupting):* I can see that. They are all being used by your fears.

PAUL: I feel like I'm slowly emerging from the secret I've been keeping from my shadow all these years. How many secrets about myself are you keeping from me damn you?

SELF-CONFIDENCE: Only the secrets for which you need to know their answer to be able to find the password that will unlock the reason you think that you belong more to the part of your sadness which believes that your past owes it a lot, than to the part of your happiness which believes that the moment it's born it is already in debt to your future.

PAUL: I sense that the important questions my life wants to ask me live in parts of my mind that no longer support me and are not willing to ever fight for me again.

SELF-CONFIDENCE: How much sunshine do you think can fit in a single "I don't know"?

PAUL: I'll be able to answer you when I regain the intellectual property rights to my silence.

SELF-CONFIDENCE: More likely when you find the courage to walk into the middle of the firing range your lies use to practice their ambiguity, dig in your heels and, raising your arms up high, start shouting as loudly as you can the name of the truth you have betrayed more than any other in your life.

PAUL: I don't know any more if I can shout, shout as hard as I can, "I am proud to be more stupid than my self-confidence" to anyone who wants to listen.

SELF-CONFIDENCE: See if you can shred into a thousand pieces the various disguises you constantly try to put on me, so you can find out if you really believe what you just said.

PAUL: So I can put on the gorgeous noose you have made for me out of the thousands of little lies that never had the opportunity to learn how to tell bigger lies? It is so frustrating, almost everytime they see me sitting alone, listless, not knowing what to do, to watch them come near me and sit next to me, so I can teach them how to become better at what they do.

SELF-CONFIDENCE: I am not going to be the one who will install you in the driver's seat of your misery's favorite toy, you will put yourself there. You should know that even your biggest lies are more afraid of you than your smallest truth is.

PAUL: Why should I be so afraid of my lies?

SELF-CONFIDENCE: Don't interrupt me. It is not me, after all, who every night proposes marriage to the steepest downhill in your life, the one which has already rejected you a thousand times. It is not me that rushes every midnight before going to sleep to put my arms around my daily defeats, to hide them so that my ego won't have time to see them before I can explain them to him in a way that will cause him the least pain possible. So, step aside and let your next heartbeat pass first through your truth and then through the rest of your body, so it can show you how much more than you think you belong to the echo left behind by your hopes when they find the courage to confess to you that they don't want to be yours anymore.

PAUL: Maybe they don't want to be hopes anymore…

SELF-CONFIDENCE: Have you ever wondered whether people would need to wear wigs in a world with no mirrors?

PAUL: Ah, a world without mirrors. How wonderful, how nice…

SELF-CONFIDENCE: You would like that, wouldn't you? It would be really convenient, wouldn't it?

PAUL: Yes, yes, it would be great…You should know, however, that I respect my image.

SELF-CONFIDENCE: You don't respect what it has to say to you, though.

PAUL: What do you mean?

SELF-CONFIDENCE: You don't respect your image. You don't trust it. You don't respect your lies. You can't afford their maintenance costs. You don't respect your truth. You are just afraid of her.

PAUL: What…

SELF-CONFIDENCE *(Raising her hand to stop him from speaking)*: What do you think your image does when you don't force it to proclaim to everyone around you how much you are really worth? What do you think it does during the hours it's left all alone, the hours during which to find the truth, any truth, it is forced to peel away from you and go sit a few feet away, where the echo of the blinding floodlights and phony compliments you use to make your world seem less empty, less useless than it is, fades out?

PAUL: Don't confuse me with images and echoes, I'm just living a life driving my lies to where they want to go.

SELF-CONFIDENCE: How many hours of your life have you wasted, though, wandering in the echo of the despicable compliments which you often draw like a gun from your mouth's holster to quickly kill the kind of truth you just decided that you no longer want to represent you?

PAUL: Quite a few. You know, though, that on the surface of the lies of others I often discover the weaknesses of my own.

SELF-CONFIDENCE: Your truth was never meant for speed readers.

PAUL: Allow me to be fascinated by my truth's demonstrations of strength. Even though they might not be as innocent as I often think, they are good for me, they are such a relief…

SELF-CONFIDENCE: You really like to use your enormous mental sledgehammer to smash every side of the lies you tell your ego to keep him artificially happy, to keep him as far away as possible from your next sorrow, which doesn't stop looking at you from the least illuminated corner of your life, winking at you mischievously. You furiously pound them for hours, until you crush them into thousands of little pieces, trying to find in the debris even the smallest token of your own identity.

PAUL: In this token I found the part of my soul that kept looking for me all these years.

SELF-CONFIDENCE: Tell me, how do you feel each time your conscience decides to lend you to one of your selves you would never want to use again?

PAUL: Don't make me feel like the amateur locksmith of every word I utter, when I can't even figure out the meaning I tried to put in it. That role doesn't suit me. Don't ask me to abandon my own identity, the person I am, the one I want to become, at the mercy of the decision that for days now has been hiding in the harshest, most uncompromising word I cannot confess to myself that the time has come for me to push out of my mouth and let the world know what I am so afraid of. Don't do that to me. I won't have any evidence left after that to prove to myself that I am still who I think I am.

SELF-CONFIDENCE: I'd really love it if every person's passport had two pages, on one of which the holder himself could write down everything he fears and on the other everything he hopes for!

PAUL (*He doesn't respond*)...

SELF-CONFIDENCE: Don't expect, though, to rediscover through the answers your silence will give me, the part of yourself that won't talk to you anymore.

PAUL: Don't you believe that a man's memory is the diary of his silences?

SELF-CONFIDENCE: No, it is the chronicle of the things his silences never told him.

PAUL: If that is so, what is a memory's ulterior motive?

SELF-CONFIDENCE: To make you seem more sure of yourself than you really are, by making the part of your past where more of your character flaws live compared to any other traits of yours, seem more obscure than it actually is.

PAUL: I cannot escape what I cannot catch up to. I can't even escape what I can never make my own. Bring me a nakedness to wear, bring me an embrace to help me understand what my compassion is trying to tell me, bring me an end to learn how to begin, bring me a joy to teach me how to steal my own courage from my next cowardice.

SELF-CONFIDENCE: I can now hear clearly what your most ambitious injury screams from inside you.

PAUL: What do you want me to do? That's all my mistakes can remember from my past.

SELF-CONFIDENCE: I don't know if you are able to see your shortcomings running all together as hard as they can to get away from the fog which those wounds of yours that still want to collaborate with your ego to produce a better tomorrow just finished making.

PAUL: A memory's end never recognizes a sorrow's beginning.

SELF-CONFIDENCE: I would say that the end of a memory never recognizes the onset of a fog whose owner loves it more than any other. After all, you can fall into a truth even when you are not standing close to it.

PAUL: And injure yourself?

SELF-CONFIDENCE: No, free yourself.

PAUL: Well, I don't need that. Over the years I learned how to lock myself out of my happiness without ever having asked my sorrow for her key.

SELF-CONFIDENCE: Two tomorrows are ready, any time you ask them, to paint the thoughts you are unable to think on your mind's most ambitious corner.

PAUL: Stop. You make me feel as if my future managed just now to get behind my back using an amazing dance move. I'm not sure if today is the day my future intends to announce to me at which point in my life it wishes to begin. Now that I think of it, I am afraid that these two "tomorrows" you are talking about are ready to make love in my mind as provocatively as they can, to force me to notice them and realize what they are trying to tell me.

SELF-CONFIDENCE: I think it's time you charged your optimism for a while. I see its batteries are low. Maybe the time has come for you to realize that cowardice can easier sell a beginning than buy an ending.

PAUL: I will try not to forget that a beginning is closer to an end than cowardice is to courage.

SELF-CONFIDENCE: Perhaps…

PAUL: I can't see clearly the price I have to pay to end the transaction with the questions I want to ask myself without being overheard by the guilt tomorrow will demand of me to surrender to it so it will let me enter it. I would gladly exchange ten joyful moments I experienced in the past with the melancholy that's been hounding me for some time now, trying to grab me from inside the next word I utter.

SELF-CONFIDENCE: How insignificant all your old happy moments seem when you are sad! Each time you are afraid to free yourself from your sorrow, you end up enslaving yourself to the minute you are experiencing, as if your happiness is constantly obliged to be indebted to the misery which every minute of your life demands to have in it.

PAUL: A slave of every moment I live… Which other part of me should I drag to the altar of my next happiness for sacrifice to satisfy my most insatiable sorrow*s*? I can't stand seeing them across from me smacking their lips while watching me struggle to walk among the mines my own memory has laid in the next hour of my life. Come, help me! Don't sit around, come on, and throw yourself between me and the coming sorrow. Help me find the courage to raise my mental stature in opposition to that disgusting "maybe" I constantly use myself which, not knowing out of what material to build it, I foolishly keep on making out of the strongest steel.

SELF-CONFIDENCE: After making a U-turn and standing up straight, your shadow has passed over your body and is trying to get into the next minute of your life ahead of you. Time no longer wants to sit next to you and has started walking alone in your future, trying to find a spot next to your truth to lie down.

PAUL: What are you telling me, that it's time for me to stay as long as it takes across from me and start making a beginning from scratch?

SELF-CONFIDENCE: I am telling you that every night, before you rejoin the soul you left at home in the morning while leaving to go to work, you should check how many parts of hers you left as collateral with the next step in your life you wish to climb, so that it will grant you its permission to set your foot on it.

PAUL: Dear God, is there a captain who knows how to shipwreck the right way?

SELF-CONFIDENCE: You mean, is there a captain who knows how to shipwreck his ship so it won't look like he did it intentionally?

PAUL: How the hell do you manage everytime to arrive at the time of day when I finally find enough courage in me to go and stand in the worst lit corner of my mind, waiting to welcome the waste my ego has started dumping inside it?

SELF-CONFIDENCE: For some time now you've made me wait at the crossing of your sorrow with that November night, the one winter came on the most beautiful day of summer and planted in the middle of your greatest joy to make you stop hoping that it won't come this year. Silence is not just the death of a word, it's also the death of a self-confidence.

PAUL: Are you trying to tell me that only those who don't know how to properly hope can dream?

SELF-CONFIDENCE: A person cannot quarrel with his future without quarreling with his favorite version of his past as well, the one his self-confidence has deliberately forgotten in the most visible spot of his memory. Is it time, perhaps, for you to realize that you may have a second infinity in you which operates only when the first one is not working anymore?

PAUL: I am sure that I often have a second sorrow inside me which operates only when the first one breaks down.

SELF-CONFIDENCE: We are saying almost the same thing.

PAUL: You make me feel as if each time I talk to you, I end up talking to my fittest shortcomings at the same time. You make me feel as if I am the greediest wastebasket there's ever been.

SELF-CONFIDENCE: Have you ever wondered why everytime you have a discussion with your character flaws you insist on just you talking, while everytime you converse with your good qualities you only want to listen? Why do you want so much to be what is left of your mind once you remove your most important thoughts?

PAUL: I won't answer you. I will let my guilt answer you, by telling you about those parts of hers that never managed to convince me that they are mine.

SELF-CONFIDENCE: Take a flying leap and get into whatever cannot mentally fit in your head anymore. The moment you start looking, even fleetingly, at the backup truth of your life, you will never be able to look again at your main one. You know, every semi-basement learns over time to understand what the shadows cast by the bodies of passersby hide in them when they walk in front of it, even if it can only see half of them.

PAUL: Every morning I sit at a desk across from my past and try to teach it a new truth.

SELF-CONFIDENCE: One of those truths you are already familiar with or the ones you learn more and more about while you are telling them? Or are they, perhaps, the truths you don't know but simply feel?

PAUL: Why are you asking me that? You know that by just trying to feel, I ended up discovering from what material my soul is made of.

SELF-CONFIDENCE: Why do you keep asking your next mistake, which will agree with what you just said, to fall in love with you?

PAUL: My next mistake has already started writing what it thinks about me on the back side of my next decision.

SELF-CONFIDENCE: I can see that.

PAUL: Where?

SELF-CONFIDENCE: On the main entrance of your sorrow I see your mistake holding a sign that says: "Seats available, please come in".

PAUL: I don't like seeing main entrances anymore, just exits, only exits…Ambiguity of mine, please move aside and let me go by. Self-confidence of mine, can you please change something on me and make my life a bit easier? While I am struggling to cope with the doubts I feel overwhelming me, with the corner of my eye I see my truth begin constructing a huge emergency exit in the part of my reality I no longer have access to.

SELF-CONFIDENCE: Yes, at the end of the long hallway whose walls are painted an eerie dark-pink color and are covered on the left with dozens of your photographs in which you are hugging a different old guilt of yours, while on the right, as you move along, there are photographs of yourself arm in arm with all the major mistakes you made in your life. When you reach the end of the hallway, you open the emergency exit you were talking about and see your next decision, almost beside herself, applauding you wildly.

PAUL: Remind me when tomorrow isn't looking to show you some of my old injuries. By God, there are times when I feel that I first taught my eyes how to cry and then how to see.

SELF-CONFIDENCE: You know, you must first endure to walk to the end of a soul before you get to meet her beginning.

PAUL: What do you mean?

SELF-CONFIDENCE: Look inside you to find which part of your soul is already talking to your next mistake, without you being able to hear what they say. Look for the parts of her back side that are reflected on the surface of the next minute of your life when you look at her with you logic's engine turned off.

PAUL: Listening to you speak, I feel my logic running panic-stricken to switch on all the lights in my mind, so she'll be able to see, to realize its dimensions.

SELF-CONFIDENCE: If you want to do something for yourself, go get the biggest mistakes you made in your life from the deepest point of the abyss where you nailed them so they won't be able to reach the surface of your daily routine and force you to admit that they are yours. Grab them by the neck and start washing them off one by one in the sink your honesty uses to clean your future before she hands it to you to wear.

PAUL: I feel as if every day I grow older by throwing behind me a piece of my future that I think I won't need and by adding a piece of yesterday's truth, to which I instantly pledge to never part with it.

SELF-CONFIDENCE: Do you, perhaps, also add the piece of truth your past would have liked to have produced alone, without any help from you?

PAUL: Perhaps, perhaps…

SELF-CONFIDENCE: If someone tells you that a day can have two dawns don't believe him.

PAUL: Should I believe him, though, if he says that there won't be a sunset tonight, because the sun spent all his energy illuminating the world all day and, exhausted, took off early from work?

SELF-CONFIDENCE: Yes, you should.

PAUL: The damn past has just planted inside me, in a spot I cannot easily locate, a brand new slavery, so it may use it whenever it needs it again in the future.

SELF-CONFIDENCE: Now I understand how you train your cowardice to always walk a step ahead of your every dream. Don't let her convince you, though, that it's time to cut the dream in half, in order to find out how it ends. It's not worth it. If you want to do something useful, try to find out who you are by picking up a handful of the dust you raised yourself while walking through yesterday and bring it very close to your face to see which pieces of yourself are still in it.

PAUL: Are you telling me to start creating a day out of all that I was not yesterday?

SELF-CONFIDENCE: Try to create a tomorrow out of all that you didn't manage to become yesterday.

PAUL: That's not easy…

SELF-CONFIDENCE: Let me help you. Can you, please, not believe what a night tells you before you realize how much darker than you those darknesses in your life that admire you want to be?

PAUL: I would give anything to know how to get rid of the trash I've been collecting inside me all these years. It's so disappointing to see it rot for quite a while on my soul's floor, making any emotion of hers smell really bad everytime it comes out of her. I feel as if the emotional trash from my previous day arrives all at once every morning and leaves my next decision on my bedside table, so I can pick it up and take it with me wherever I go.

SELF-CONFIDENCE: Sure, sure… It will convince you to walk all day, letting you think that you alone decide which way to go, until your day taps you on the shoulder and orders you to stop at the spot your emotional trash picked to force you to meet the side of your reality that hates you more than it admires you.

PAUL: And you, damn you, will instantly grab the only rainbow that still lives inside me by its most frightened end and will start hitting me with it all over my body, to see for how long I will be able to take a beating without calling my truth to rush over to save me, how long I will endure your blows without starting to draw in breaths borrowed from the oxygen that my conscience has long been hiding inside the one phrase which my self-awareness has never let me utter.

SELF-CONFIDENCE: Have you ever wondered whether by accidentally stumbling on who you are, you end up falling on what you are afraid you will become?

PAUL: Stop handcuffing tomorrow; I don't need your help, I can do it by myself.

SELF-CONFIDENCE: I don't want to do that, I simply want to tell you that the road to the oasis you are looking for runs through the desert you are already crossing. Face it. There is no oasis where there's no desert. After all, for years now I have agreed with my mistakes to let them live only in houses they themselves have built.

PAUL: You wouldn't believe how often I think that I am the only human being in the world who lives in an oasis which chose, out of all the available types of land, to be surrounded by desert.

SELF-CONFIDENCE: Because I know you well, I'd guess that your oasis has chosen to place its desert at its center.

PAUL: Now that we've determined how deep my abyss is, tell me, what's the difference between your mistakes and mine?

SELF-CONFIDENCE: Why don't you tell me?

PAUL *(Confused, he rests his head on his hands):* I feel that a lie has been following me around for days now. The cursed thing demands to negotiate with my future on my behalf, without me being there. Dear God, why must there always be a full stop lurking at the edge of my self-confidence that takes orders only from my cowardice and not from me?

SELF-CONFIDENCE: Because you personally arm the hand of your most ambitious defeatism and then order it to start cutting the barbed wire you used to enclose all the insecurities you have in your soul. You want so much to set them free so they can wander all through your life and start wrecking it!

PAUL: But...

SELF-CONFIDENCE: How did you manage, you incredible man, to build a whole life out of your own doubts?

PAUL: By learning how to share my mistakes with the echo my authenticity produces when she passes through my most dangerous delusions.

SELF-CONFIDENCE: I think it's time you admitted that you recognized what you are afraid to think about in what you just said.

PAUL: Why do you want to coat with rust everything I'm trying to learn from scratch how to feel properly? Why do you want to make me leaf through the book of my insecurities, knowing that I'm still not ready to face them? How the hell do you manage every day to give birth to a slavery in the middle of my freedom, especially knowing that if I find myself in an incredibly beautiful place that includes a cell -yet lets me know at the same time that I am free to go wherever I want- I will run as fast as I can to lock myself up in it?

SELF-CONFIDENCE: The certainty of slavery is great and even greater is the uncertainty of freedom.

PAUL: But...

SELF-CONFIDENCE: It's also a great quality for a man to not do his best, among all the places in his life, to crawl and lock himself up in the only cell given to him by any triumph of his that never believed in him.

PAUL: I always felt subjugated by the spelling my freedom chooses to write the questions she avoids asking me on the margin of my smallest truth, so I won't be able to easily discover them. *(Pause)* Soul of mine, what color is your rust? What color is your light? What color is your biggest doubt? Tell me, why must there be so many days when even if I am able to touch all three of them with my own eyes, I still cannot see it.

SELF-CONFIDENCE: The perfection that wants to swing open only towards the side where her owner's good qualities permanently live has no front entrance.

PAUL: Please, don't make me look among the various kinds of logic I use from time to time to find the pieces of my optimism that contain the first perfect step I have had at my disposal for years now.

SELF-CONFIDENCE: You know, there are truths that are built in such a way that they don't necessarily want what's best for their owners.

PAUL: My fears no longer coincide with the fears of my courage. I feel as if my inadequacy and my perfection have grabbed me by the throat and are forcing me to umpire the duel they both insist on starting right away.

SELF-CONFIDENCE: Have you ever wondered how much your perfection hates you?

PAUL: What a shame. I always thought she was in love with me.

SELF-CONFIDENCE: Look around you. The thousands of realities which you concocted yourself so you won't be able to recognize among them the one you are experiencing each time, have become permanent spectators in the Coliseum of your life and right now, one after the other, they are turning their thumbs down.

PAUL: Yes I know them, I know these minor defeats my perfection is in the habit of giving birth to inside me after every triumph, without asking me.

SELF-CONFIDENCE: Is it time you kneeled before your mind, hoping you might convince it to pity you and bend down to whisper in your ear all about how your characters flaws really behave?

PAUL: Don't ask me to lend you the last May living inside me, I couldn't bear parting with it.

SELF-CONFIDENCE: That's the reason every loneliness wants to conceal the success of a failure inside her.

PAUL: You make me feel that I belong to the giant "thank-you" I owe to what is left of my success if I remove the luck that helped me achieve it. The game my damn luck plays with me is so indecent. Sitting between my self-criticism and my success, winking at me mischievously, she tells at me: "Don't you dare believe in any of these two if you don't believe in me first!"

SELF-CONFIDENCE: Then what did you do?

PAUL: Already entangled, I started wrapping the version of myself I will use tomorrow in the least amount of compassion I always ought to have, according to the promises I made to the part of my courage inside which, no matter how hard I searched, I never managed to find the owner's manual of my soul.

SELF-CONFIDENCE: Why don't you try to unwrap your intelligence from inside the honesty of your thoughts and see what happens. *(Pause)* You are asking me for a lot! You are asking me so many times in the same day to take you by the hand and lead you to the point in your life where the ruins from different periods of hers insist on meeting each other, so they can-explain their own dreams, and after standing me upright in the middle, you force them to pass before me one by one so I can introduce myself to them. *(Pause)* Which part of your soul remains undefeated after so many battles, which one can look you in the eyes and say to you, after the many times you have managed to enslave it, that it is still truly free?

PAUL: I don't know…When I learned how to calculate, I stopped counting. When I learned how to smile, I stopped being afraid. When I learned to understand what my cowardice wants from me, I stopped retreating. How much longer will I be able to write the apologies I owe myself on those pages of my melancholy that will never be read? How much longer will I pretend that I am not dominated by the blurry memories and the cardboard optimism I let my ambiguity produce in order to protect me from the secrets I keep from the love I have for the midnight which I still haven't figured out which piece of myself it is that it wants so much to give me as a gift?

SELF-CONFIDENCE: Till you realize that in every word you utter, in every action of yours, your feelings of guilt have already managed to stick their most combat ready version -the one which will attack you the second it sees you relaxing, letting your guard down.

PAUL: Sometimes I feel that my damn feelings of guilt have produced over time their own conscience, which really wants to set up interrogation rooms right at the edge of every act of mine, every word of mine, so they can find ways to prosecute me, not just once in a while, but constantly.

SELF-CONFIDENCE: How convenient it would be if guilt was self-repealing!

PAUL: You mean if it had an expiration date?

SELF-CONFIDENCE: Don't try for the second time during the same conversation to scale the peak of your abyss. Once is enough to keep your defeatism happy. Please don't use all the mistakes at your disposal today. Leave some for tomorrow…

PAUL: You know, there are no insensitive hearts, just hearts that don't find it profitable anymore to feel.

SELF-CONFIDENCE: Stop being fascinated by every spot in your heart you don't know what you have to do to defeat it and start looking right away for the spot in her where you have hidden your loudest scream tonight. Don't hesitate to hug it as tightly as you can, just in case you manage to obtain some of the freedom, the passion it has in it.

PAUL: Throughout my life I always served the part of my meanness I didn't know how to defend myself from.

SELF-CONFIDENCE: Is it, perhaps, time for you to sit across from your uniqueness so that together you can check what your common interests are?

PAUL: Damn you, I know where you are taking this. You want to once again make me try to find out if I have more common interests with the major victories in my life that with my great defeats.

SELF-CONFIDENCE: Yes, especially the ones that made you believe that to conquer them you don't have to buy off your inadequacy from the side of your conscience that pretends to look elsewhere everytime you go to ask her for a favor. It's amazing how much man likes to brag about those character traits of his for which he doesn't know how to be ashamed of!

PAUL: What are you trying to say, that my success is ready to succeed without me?

SELF-CONFIDENCE: Do you realize that the very same words your victories bent down and whispered in your ear just seconds after you won, you had already confided to them yourself long ago in a moment of weakness? Do you ever wonder if you can fit in the same mind as every new victory you achieve?

PAUL: Please don't make the permanent winter that lives in the favorite part of my body unbutton its shirt to show me what it is made of.

SELF-CONFIDENCE: Why do you avoid…

PAUL: Because the first time a soul decides to throw off her the disguise she used for years to hide from the authenticity of her owner, she should not do it in front of all the gold medals her cowardice won for defeating his own happiness. She should do this when she's alone, when there's no one else around to see the depth of each wound she suffered in order to survive. Don't forget that there will always be a neglected sadness lying about, to which no one will have ever paid any attention, sitting a hesitation away from every person pretending he never ordered her.

SELF-CONFIDENCE: Please go sit right next to any thought you have right this moment in your mind that doesn't want to hurt you.

PAUL: Do you know that everytime I win, I end up inheriting another piece of my mind's nakedness from the most invisible insecurity I have ever felt?

SELF-CONFIDENCE: Sometimes, hearing you talk, I have the impression that you never want to get a passing grade from your sorrow, you never want to graduate from her.

PAUL: My age today is more ready than ever to discover again the part of my enthusiasm I didn't get a chance to give to my adolescence before reality came and grabbed it from my own hands.

SELF-CONFIDENCE: I think that, no matter how hard you try, you will never be able to defeat your age, if first you don't understand what your memory seeks from your future.

PAUL: Do you know that this is exactly the kind of question

that the first question I have to ask my soul each time the two of us manage to be all alone refuses to answer?

SELF-CONFIDENCE: Everything small demands to have something smaller next to it.

PAUL: Do you mean to say that every cowardice would like to have a bigger cowardice next to her?

SELF-CONFIDENCE: I think you must stop trying to find the kind of misery that exactly fits your size today.

PAUL: Do you mean the size of my joy today? *(Pause)* Please let me discover on my own that there is something more useless that uselessness.

SELF-CONFIDENCE: Close the door of the night you intentionally left open, because I see thousands of melodies returning to your mind, melodies which hide a strange sound inside them, the sound emanating from those old dreams of yours you never managed to dream.

PAUL: I think it's time for my self-awareness to stop keeping notes and bury them as fast as she can in the deepest spot of my mind, so that I won't ever find them again.

SELF-CONFIDENCE: Stop fighting tooth and nail to not hear the scream which your silence has long since been carrying within her. Unlock the spring from everything you cannot feel, no matter how hard you try, and start reading the letter the poor first day of winter wrote to you just before it surrendered to its own defeatism.

PAUL: You've told me before. I don't know how I'm going to do this ...

SELF-CONFIDENCE: Tear a spring day in two, to try to find the notes your happiness left for you long ago.

PAUL: How the hell can my deepest melancholy insist on living in the shallowest part of my soul?

SELF-CONFIDENCE: She lives there because she likes to shipwreck frequently. Can you please try to find the first words you want to utter in the body of your last silence?

PAUL: Self-confidence of mine, help me transfuse blood from one of my dreams to another. I need to, I really do... Why, everytime I argue with myself, does it take me an hour to start realizing what I wanted to say to begin with? Why, everytime I argue with someone else, do I start realizing how stupid what I expected to gain from the fight actually is only after I begin to look through the wreckage our two egos leave behind while we are talking,? After all this quarreling, after all this bitterness, how many dimensions of the different realities, which my rage is simultaneously negotiating with on my behalf, can I host inside me at the same time?

SELF-CONFIDENCE: As many as the version of your cowardice that you will use tomorrow allows you to have. Either way, as you know, you can cash in any of your delusions whenever you want at the pawnshop your conscience has opened on the sidewalk just across the street from your ego.

PAUL: Please don't involve my conscience in this. You know that the opinion she will have of me tomorrow is much more important to me than any victory that I am trying to convince to be mine just for today so that I will be able to make myself feel better.

SELF-CONFIDENCE: If you look more carefully, I am sure that you will find the part of your past that will allow you to perpetually recycle it until you make it look like something that will offer you the new kind of happiness you always wanted.

PAUL: I know, I know… It's not life that brings happiness, it's kindness.

SELF-CONFIDENCE: I'm glad you remember what I've told you.

PAUL: How can I forget when there's an equally large part of my conscience that reminds me daily?

SELF-CONFIDENCE: You mean there's a part of her that refuses to become part of your meanness?

PAUL: No, I'm talking about the section of hers which refuses to become part of the future I want.

SELF-CONFIDENCE: Do you know when this happens?

PAUL: No, I don't.

SELF-CONFIDENCE: When a person starts becoming the archeologist of his own silence, digging to find in the words that were buried in the ruins it occasionally left in the souls of the people he loved those dreams which, having traveled all over the world on his behalf, never dared to return to him so they could tell his soul what they saw, what they felt.

PAUL: It's really incredible how we people ultimately end up dancing with an effigy of our past, which we buried ourselves as deep as we could in our future so it will never be able to discover it ahead of us.

SELF-CONFIDENCE: Who are you kidding! Since you are able to bury whole sunbeams in your sorrow, don't you think that if you wanted to, you could also bury a tiny part of your past in your future?

PAUL *(Shaking his head):* Man is a huge miracle factory, often a factory that produces stillborn miracles.

SELF-CONFIDENCE: Especially after he realizes that he is the blackest darkness there is in the world.

PAUL: Man may even be the only darkness that has found a way to survive amid its own light. *(His Self-Confidence does not reply)* I really like seeing you projected on the huge screen which the questions that refuse to be asked have set up in my mind's main square to show the commercial my inadequacy has prepared about myself.

SELF-CONFIDENCE: Is it, perhaps, time for you to visit the pawnshop of the main sorrow in your life and try once again to buy even one of the happinesses you had previously sold to your ambiguity?

PAUL: Is this, perhaps, the redeeming birth of a word whose owner doesn't ever want to know that it's been living secretly inside him for years?

SELF-CONFIDENCE: Can you speak with a man's current sorrow without simultaneously speaking with his next one?

PAUL: Why, can you speak with his previous sorrow without speaking with his next mistake at the same time? *(Pause)* For that matter, can you speak with his happiness for hours without being forced at some point to speak with the questions his adolescence left forever unanswered?

SELF-CONFIDENCE: And God came and gave mankind a gigantic zero, to help people devise a new way to feel sad…

PAUL: As if we don't have enough…

SELF-CONFIDENCE: There are many you still don't know about…

PAUL: That's why the first thing a truth does when she's born is to anxiously rush to start constructing her own silence, before the most significant word her owner has in his mind gets a chance to craft it ahead of her.

SELF-CONFIDENCE: Today all fairytales will be asked to first cross the entire truth contained in the life of their owners and then they will open their mouths to confide to them all that the part of their own life they fear most refuses to tell them.

PAUL: And all the self-awarenesses will hide whatever they don't understand deep in their guilt, so that…

SELF-CONFIDENCE: …so that egos won't start asking the questions that rush to conceal the answers as best they can, before they start pretending that they are searching for them.

PAUL: Are these the bad checks a truth leaves behind when the time comes for her owner to ask her to pay the bill of his own past, the one he has intentionally left unpaid?

SELF-CONFIDENCE: Don't start throwing off your shackles before you realize what freedom means to you.

PAUL: The tremendous insecurity that tomorrow feels just caught me tightly in its grasp. I can feel it. It will force me to sit on its lap and then, using my self-criticism's sharpest edge, it will show me how to tear my shadow in two.

SELF-CONFIDENCE: Why don't you ask it if this is the way a person learns how to protect his mistakes from his own future?

PAUL: Could it be that our mistakes don't actually live outside our minds, scattered randomly at various points in our future, but inside us, and the majesty of the human mind comes down to simply finding a way to not bring them into contact with its own future? Could it be that every second of our life, every decision of ours, is a stick of dynamite that suddenly appears in front of our face, challenging our self-confidence to get out of our body in the guise of a single word or a single act, and like the good flame she is, blow us into smithereens? What do you think?

SELF-CONFIDENCE: I think you are the mistake your next smile will make in not realizing out of how many tears of yours it is made.

PAUL: Egos are getting winded today, trying to climb those downhills the truths gave them as gifts a while ago. I remember that my life's ashes always came dressed as smiles to all my mind's biggest parties. Now I think a February came dressed as a June. Don't be fooled my heart! Don't be fooled, his skin might be sunburned, his flesh might be giving off steam due to the lovely hot outdoor temperature, but his innards are made of the icebergs planted in him one after the other by each day that makes up the future my adolescence never had.

SELF-CONFIDENCE: In the depths of your cowardice lives a hero who refuses to learn how to breed insecurities on your behalf.

PAUL: And not only that. He also covers parts of my conscience's surface with a kind of mirror on which, everytime I look into it, I can only see reflected the side of my face my self-criticism has crafted using only the part of its knowledge of me it has already forgotten.

SELF-CONFIDENCE: Truth is a true Spartan. The sunbeams that illuminate you today melt away before they hit your body. Once again you managed to persuade the wings that the wind will use to fly, to hide within them those secrets of yours that make them too heavy, unable to lift you off the ground.

PAUL: Do you think this is the price Paradise will ask of me to leave me outside?

SELF-CONFIDENCE: To find the answer, change your sorrow's last name.

PAUL: It doesn't really matter, since my ambiguity uses different names everytime she travels, names she refuses to share with me.

SELF-CONFIDENCE: Don't worry, a day will come when you won't be able, no matter how carefully you look, to recognize yourself among your ashes!

PAUL: I am afraid that there will come a day when I won't be able to recognize the only flame that belongs to me amid the huge fire I will have lit to burn my character flaws. I don't know, I might be able -if I manage to do something I've never done before- to stand before the gifts my own ashes won't stop bringing me and find the strength to explain to each one why I refuse to pick it up.

SELF-CONFIDENCE: Stop digging in your happiness to try to discover the treasure of old coins your self-control has planted inside her to make you feel good about yourself.

PAUL: Sometimes I think it's not her precious coins, but the loot she stole from my serenity.

SELF-CONFIDENCE: Rich is a man who cannot turn on the lights in that room of his mind where his poverty permanently lives. How the hell did you manage to become day by day your own self's awkward broker, using nothing more than middle-age guilt to build in your mind the massive walls that separate your previous hesitation from your next step, your thoughts from your next decision? How deep inside you has your adolescence buried that freedom of yours that still knows how to be free, so you won't be able to ever find her? Have you ever wondered why, before every great battle in your life, your cowardice always tried to find out in which part of the defeat she had hidden the most effective fog you had in your arsenal?

PAUL: Because as I was growing up I learned how to increasingly sedate myself daily by swallowing another blinding defeat of old, thus exhausting my optimism more and more, forcing it to constantly go up and down carrying each loss separately to the highest point of my soul. Day by day, I became better at not being able to lose what I should never win in the first place, better at not asking questions about what I should never learn. The moment a person begins to feel that his own logic hates him, he starts dismembering by himself the light his body emanates on his behalf, tearing it in so many shreds that, no matter how hard he might try, he could never reattach them to recreate his brightness.

Can a man unwillingly forget something on purpose? I can. I can because I have ordered my shadow to not pick up all that my ego throws behind it everytime it rushes to enter my next decision ahead of me. It seems that by letting my cry beat me, I allowed my trash to create, but never own, its own trash.

SELF-CONFIDENCE: How wretched! You have grabbed in your hands an entire desert and are dragging it behind you, dragging it to water at one of the few spots in your life that hurts less than you do. Carrying it, you feel as if you carry the part of your soul that over time has become a desert, the part in which none of your emotions, even the strongest, can stand to live any longer.

PAUL: Would there be an oasis if there were no desert?

SELF-CONFIDENCE: Would there be lifejackets if there was no sea?

PAUL: Would there be kindness if there were no meanness?

SELF-CONFIDENCE: Would there be darkness if there were no light?

PAUL: How is it possible, during those moments when you feel that you no longer belong to anything, not even the desert that gave birth and raised you, to see the oasis, which for so long you thought was right before your eyes, disappear?

SELF-CONFIDENCE: Illusions are the gifts a man's ego gives to his stupidity.

PAUL: Perhaps.

SELF-CONFIDENCE: When man reaches the first crossroads in his life that has done all it can to not look like a crossroads, he feels a compelling need to look among the pieces of himself he personally tossed into tomorrow's trashcan to find out which good qualities of his still believe in him. There he will realize for the first time that he has reached the point of having to discontinue being who he is and keep what's left of his life, except for what brought him to where he is.

PAUL: I am afraid that you're right...My thoughts, before leaving my mind, often decide on their own to destroy their fingerprints. So, I ended up arming my happiness with dozens of "maybes" which came and kept me company since this morning, and then approached the dusk and hesitantly embraced it trying to convince it to pour some of its dazzlingly serene light it did not need at that time into my heart, while with my other hand I kept caressing as tenderly as I could the huge, unbearably heavy full stop which just a few minutes ago the day that's slowly ending placed a few inches ahead of all that my ego had aimed to accomplish today.

Immersed in the colors of the sunset, which every passing minute becomes weaker, sadder, I run to thrust myself into the embrace of the newborn darkness, so I can draw out of it all its purity, before it's forced, in a last attempt to save her, to wrap her around midnight and let her walk on the edge of night till daybreak. I want this purity, I really want her because she's the only one that can build me from scratch, using as raw materials everything I said during the passing day that I actually meant. I feel the hands of the sunset's last sunbeam attempting to shape me like those of a master sculptor, until I start hearing out of the sole well of honesty that can still stand to live in me -the well of a conscience that wants to learn how to forget before she remembers how to remember- my misgivings negotiating among themselves about how they will rally their forces tomorrow morning to vanquish me. *(Shouting)* Night of mine, tell me, damn you, tell me out of what material do you wish to fabricate me tonight?

SELF-CONFIDENCE: It's impressive to see a man let the part of himself he despises the most remake him from scratch using only materials which he has insisted for years that they don't live in him any longer. The damn thing comes with its various tools in its bag, spreads them on the large table in the middle of his heart and, using one material at a time, starts building him the way it wants.

PAUL: I see the loot my melancholy snatched from my time when it wasn't looking march in a bizarre parade right before me. My God, is there an abyss that sooner or later doesn't invite its owner to fall in it?

SELF-CONFIDENCE: Great guilt can fit only through the doors that no longer know how to open.

PAUL: What more is man, anyway, that the gratuity he gives his self-awareness so she will let him live another day without asking him too many questions?

SELF-CONFIDENCE: How miserable does a man feel the moment he discovers that to quench his thirst he must drink one by one those lies of his that never believed him.

PAUL: It must feel even worse when he sees the most favorite icebergs in his life argue about which one will manage to sink him first.

SELF-CONFIDENCE: What can a lie and an iceberg have in common, I wonder?

PAUL: Their love of loneliness…

SELF-CONFIDENCE: That's right.

PAUL: I feel as if tomorrow morning I will wake up having in me one more crossroads to get lost in.

SELF-CONFIDENCE: Let the tallest fence in your life explain to you what freedom means. Listen to it, it has much to tell you …

PAUL *(Raises his right hand in her direction):* You do your own thing. Let me blossom in the arms of all those things in my life I can no longer make mine, without feeling obliged to start respecting them first.

SELF-CONFIDENCE: You mean those things which, because you can't defeat them with your mind, you are trying to vanquish with your soul?

PAUL *(Sarcastically):* I thank you for all that you are doing so I will forget the reason I am trying to feel sad right now.

SELF-CONFIDENCE: Don't forget to put in your tears all that your previous sorrow ordered from you. Don't forget that you have appointed yourself the favorite servant of the steepest cliffs that live inside you, the ones that swallow up economy-class truths and spit out first-class ambiguities.

PAUL: Those sheer drops that are even more omnivorous than me?

SELF-CONFIDENCE: I am afraid so.

PAUL: Why are you hell-bent today on turning me into the collateral that time will have to deposit with my happiness to convince her to acquire me from my biggest insecurities? Why are you pushing me to enter the last drop of sweat I shed to acquire what I didn't deserve? Why do you do that, damn you? How much joy can you derive from it, anyway?

SELF-CONFIDENCE: Before you attack me, please let your tears compare their ambitions with the ambition of your happiness and when they are done, go sit for a while on the sidelines of your life accompanied only by your arrogance, and listen to what they want to confide to you.

PAUL: What will they say?

SELF-CONFIDENCE: Listen to the favor they need from you. *(Paul doesn't respond)* Why don't you say something? Stop making love to your loneliness all the time, take two steps aside and place your hands on the only emergency exit in your life whose key is held by your humility, and soon after you shall see the words you are afraid to admit are yours returning on their own to your mouth.

PAUL: Everything you are saying is being written on my forehead in capital letters. I am glad you made me feel sad, because that way I feel like I have drawn closer to the happy moments in my life which, since I never managed to understand them, I am sure that sooner rather than later I will be forced to feel.

SELF-CONFIDENCE: Your past won't be a desert anymore if today you find the strength to plant in it a single flower. *(Pause)* A tiny little flower can easily defeat an entire desert, if it realizes how strong it is.

PAUL: How?

SELF-CONFIDENCE: By making the desert start doubting itself.

PAUL: Isn't this the way that black has stopped demanding to be the night's revenge? *(His Self-Confidence does not respond)* I feel like grabbing my shadow with my right hand and tearing it in half, peeling it off my body and laying it on the questions borne by the very first phrase we exchanged today.

SELF-CONFIDENCE: Please, do it… do it …

THE END

Cover painting
There are times when I feel that I first taught my eyes how to cry and then how to see.

Back cover painting
I cannot escape what I cannot catch up to. I can't even escape what I can never make my own. Bring me a nakedness to wear, bring me an embrace to help me understand what my compassion is trying to tell me, bring me an end to learn how to begin, bring me a joy to teach me how to steal my own courage from my next cowardice.

www.ingramcontent.com/pod-product-compliance
Lightning Source LLC
Chambersburg PA
CBHW042337150426
43195CB00001B/18